30 australian ghost stories for children

To my boys, Dom and Jas, with love.
And to John and Goff, as always. LK

For Dad. GR

Random House Australia Pty Ltd
20 Alfred Street, Milsons Point, NSW 2061
http://www.randomhouse.com.au

Sydney   New York   Toronto
London   Auckland   Johannesburg

First published by Random House Australia 2004

Text copyright © see acknowledgements for individual stories
Illustrations copyright © Gregory Rogers 2004

All rights reserved. No part of this publication may be reproduced, stored in a retrieval system, or transmitted in any form or by any means, electronic, mechanical, photocopying, recording or otherwise, without the prior written permission of the publisher.

National Library of Australia
Cataloguing-in-Publication Entry

30 Australian ghost stories for children.

   For primary students.
   ISBN 0 7593 2037 3.

   1. Ghost stories, Australian. 2. Children's stories, Australian. I. Knight, Linsay, 1952- . II. Rogers, Gregory, 1957- . III. Title.

A823.08733089282

Cover illustration by Gregory Rogers
Cover and text design by Monkeyfish
Typeset in Goudy Old Style 13/16 by Midland Typesetters
Printed by Tien Wah Press (PTE) Limited, Singapore

10 9 8 7 6 5 4 3 2 1

30 australian ghost stories for children

edited by LINSAY KNIGHT
illustrated by GREGORY ROGERS

RANDOM HOUSE AUSTRALIA

CONTENTS

1. 'Invisipills' from *Just Tricking!* • Andy Griffiths • 1
2. 'Zeke and Eppie and the Headless Head Ghost' from *My Sister's a Nightmare* • Gretel Killeen • 9
3. 'Do You Want to Go With Me?' from *Cool School* • John Marsden • 13
4. 'Emily and the Ghost Ship' from *Emily Eyefinger and the Ghost Ship* • Duncan Ball • 18
5. 'Tashi and the Ghosts' from *The Big, Big, Big Book of Tashi* • Anna and Barbara Fienberg • 24
6. 'Trapped!' from *Murder on the Ghoul Bus* • Margaret Clark • 31
7. *Liar Ghost* • Goldie Alexander • 36
8. *Alistair* • Jenny Blackford • 41
9. 'Tad Drowns Again' from *Ghost Boy* • Felicity Pulman • 46
10. 'Puck Goes Home' from *A Ghost of a Chance* • Nette Hilton • 50
11. *She Just Wants to Play* • Sophie Masson • 55
12. *Dragon's Tooth* • Victor Kelleher • 59
13. *Past Lives* • Vashti Farrer • 68
14. *Fluff on the Brain* • Anita Bell • 73
15. *Voices from Beyond* • Anita Bell • 77
16. 'Birdscrap' from *Unbelievable!* • Paul Jennings • 82
17. 'The Haunting of Clayton Quinn' from *Party Animals* • Christine Harris • 91

18.	*The Scent of Violets* • Elizabeth Hutchins • 95	
19.	*Federici is not a Cat* • Edel Wignell • 101	
20.	*Dead or Alive* • Janeen Brian • 106	
21.	'The Exorcist's Club' from *Eloise* • Catherine Jinks • 112	
22.	'The Smell of Goat' from *The Binna Binna Man* • Meme McDonald and Boori Monty Pryor • 117	
23.	'A Wet, Magic Night' from *The Nargun and the Stars* • Patricia Wrightson • 121	
24.	'The White Bull' from *Shudders and Shakes* • Anne Ingram • 126	
25.	'The Black Horse of Sutton' from *Shudders and Shakes* • Anne Ingram • 129	
26.	'The Little Furry Girl' from *Playing Beatie Bow* • Ruth Park • 132	
27.	'Invisible Tea' from *The Ghost of Love Street* • Venero Armanno • 138	
28.	*Net Insanity* • Paul Collins • 143	
29.	'Flesh and Blood' from *Rowan of Rin* • Emily Rodda • 147	
30.	'Double Sorrow' from *Ghostop Book One* • Libby Hathorn • 152	

FOREWORD

For thousands of years Australian storytellers have captivated their audiences with tales of what happened to their ancestors when they died, of how the living explain the unexplainable, of the unusual happenings that take place in the Australian bush and of spooky adventures experienced by people just like themselves. Some of these stories are so silly that they make you laugh out loud and don't make the hairs on your arms stand on end, others are sad and make you cry, while the really scary ones make you sit on the edge of your seat, afraid to hear what happens next. But all these stories have one thing in common – they show the riches to be found in reading or listening to Australian wordsmiths describing what they think might happen beyond the everyday world we know and the array of ghostly creations that might be out there waiting for us to let them in.

This collection of Australian treasures shows the depth and scope of our Australian ghost story heritage. From animal ghost stories like *Past Lives, Birdscrap, A Ghost of a Chance, The White Bull* and *The Black Horse of Sutton*, to *The Nargan and the Stars* and *The Binna Binna Man*, based on storytelling traditions passed from one generation to the next by word of mouth and reworked in written down forms by passionate enthusiasts and keepers of the stories, to perennial favourites like *Playing Beatie*

Bow, Tashi and the Ghosts, Rowan of Rin, Eloise, Ghostop and Cool School, all these gems take on new life when introduced to a new generation of readers.

Also included are ghostly romps like Invisipills, My Sister's a Nightmare, Murder on the Ghoul Bus, Emily and the Ghost Ship and Net Insanity that inspire us to explore our madcap side, while The Haunting of Clayton Quinn, Fluff on the Brain, Dead or Alive and Dragon's Tooth have a twist in their tail and keep us guessing to the very end. And ghostly beings from beyond the grave, as in The Scent of Violets, Ghost Boy, Liar Ghost and The Ghost of Love Street, who interact with young people in the real world and help us explore areas of our lives we don't often talk about and can't always experience for ourselves. All these stories help enrich our lives as they nourish our creative processes and give us an understanding of the world around us.

And there are stories that have never been collected before. Some of these, like The Scent of Violets, Federici is Not a Cat, Alistair and Voices From Beyond, have been treasured by their authors and waiting for the right moment to materialise, while others, like She Just Wants to Play, were specially written for this collection

But most importantly, all the stories collected here will inspire young readers to seek and find their own stories of the supernatural – the important ones that shape and change their lives – the ones they just can't wait to write down and share with others. So happy reading!

Linsay Knight

INVISIPILLS

1

From *Just Tricking!*
ANDY GRIFFITHS

Mrs Wharton is stomping around the library. She's telling kids off for talking. She's telling kids off for leaning back on their chairs. She's practically telling kids off for breathing. You name it, and she's telling them off for it.

I reckon she's wasted as a librarian. Mrs Wharton should have been the governor of a high-security prison. That'd be one prison where they wouldn't have to worry about the prisoners talking, leaning back on their chairs or returning their library books late.

The only person Mrs Wharton has not told off so far this lesson is me. That's because I'm working so hard. It's pretty rare for me to work this hard, but I have a big assignment on Antarctic explorers due on Monday. It's worth 50 per cent of our end of year mark and I've only just started it.

The trouble is, Danny is sitting at the desk next to mine and he keeps going on and on about how he wants to be invisible. He won't shut up. He's been talking about it for weeks now. Normally, I wouldn't mind, but I don't want to risk getting kicked out of the library because I need to use the Internet.

'Psst! Andy!' says Danny.

'Shhh!' I say to him. 'Do you want to get us kicked out?'

'No,' he says, 'just tell me what you reckon. If I got a can of spray-paint and painted myself pink and painted my whole room pink and everything in it pink – do you think I'd be invisible then?'

'Well, maybe,' I whisper. 'As long as you stayed in your room. But once you left, you'd be a bit conspicuous.'

'Oh,' he says.

He's quiet for a few seconds. Then he leans over again. 'Psst!'

'What!?' I say. I'm getting really impatient.

'What does "conspicuous" mean?'

'It means you'd stand out like a pimple on a pumpkin! Now would you shut up and do some work – and stop interrupting me!'

'Yeah, sorry, mate,' he says. 'But honestly, do you reckon it would work?'

'For the last time, shut up!'

I reach into my pencil case for a lolly. Well, they're *supposed* to be lollies. They're really just those little multi-coloured balls with no taste. Nobody likes them, except three-year-olds – and that's only because they don't know any better. I'm only eating them because they were a present from my granny. It would have been rude to throw them away.

I crunch one between my teeth.

Danny leans over.

'What are those?' he says.

Suddenly I have an idea of how to get rid of him.

Mrs Wharton is up at the loans counter checking out some books. This gives me a few minutes.

'Danny, what would you say if I had a way of really making you invisible?'

'How?'

I pass him the tube of lollies.

'I was waiting until your birthday to give you these, but since you want to be invisible so badly, you might as well have them now.'

'What are they?" he says.

'They're invisipills. They make you invisible.'

'For real?'

'Absolutely.'

'Where'd you get them?' he says.

'I made them in science. I got a recipe off the Net.'

Danny hits his head with his hand. 'Oh, man! Why didn't I think of that! Which site?'

'I'd rather not say. The recipe was smuggled out of the Pentagon. Top-secret stuff. I could get into a lot of trouble if I'm caught.'

'Have you tried them?'

'Yep.'

'And?'

'They're pretty amazing. One pill will make you completely invisible for about half an hour.'

'Wow!' How come you didn't tell me?'

'Like I said, I was keeping it for a surprise for your birthday.'

'Can I try one?'

'Sure. Just one, though. They're pretty powerful. And you've got to promise me one thing.'

'What?' says Danny.

'That after you've taken it you'll go outside and let me work.'

'No problem,' he says.

He takes a lolly from the tube.

His eyes are wide as he puts it onto his tongue, closes his mouth and swallows.

'Well?' he says. 'Am I invisible?'

'Not yet,' I say. 'It takes a few minutes.'

Danny's holding his hands out in front of him, fingers out-stretched.

'Have I faded even a little bit?' he says. 'What do you reckon?'

I screw up my eyes, pretending to study him.

'Yes – definitely!' I say. 'No doubt about it.'

'Cool!' he says.

I glance up. Mrs Wharton has finished at the loans counter and is prowling the library again.

'You're fading fast now,' I say. 'I can hardly see you.'

'No I'm not,' he says. 'I can still see me as clear as anything.'

'Yeah – you're meant to, you dork. That's the way the pills are designed. You can see yourself, but nobody can see you. If you couldn't see yourself, you wouldn't know where you were and you'd get lost.'

'Oh, I get it,' he says. 'So, am I invisible yet?'

'Where are you?'

'I'm right here!'

'No you're not. Not as far as I can see. Your chair is empty.'

'Can you hear me?'

'Yes. Now go outside! Remember our deal?'

'Okay,' says Danny. 'I'm outa here!'

Danny gets up out of his seat and walks off. Mrs Wharton is coming slowly towards me.

I go back to my assignment and do my best imitation of a serious student.

Just as she's walking past my desk I hear the most enormous belch. It's so loud it practically rocks the foundations of the library.

For a moment I think it was Mrs Wharton. But that – of course – is ridiculous. Only Danny can do them that loud.

I look around. Sure enough, Danny is killing himself laughing in the isle.

Mrs Wharton stops.

'Excuse me!' she says. 'Was that you?'

'No, Mrs Wharton,' I say.

'Then who was it, pray tell? A ghost?'

'I don't know, Mrs Wharton. But it wasn't me.'

'I don't believe you. What are those?' she says, pointing at the lollies, which Danny has thoughtfully left sitting on my desk in full view.

'Um . . . lollies, Mrs Wharton.'

'I presume you know the rule about eating in the library.'

'Yes, Mrs Wharton.'

'And you know that it specifically excludes chewing gum, bubble gum *and* lollies?'

'Yes, Mrs Wharton. I'll get rid of them.'

'No you won't,' she says, '*I* will.'

She holds out her hand. I pick up the tube and give it to her. Little does she realise that she's doing me a big favour.

She walks up the aisle without another word.

That was close. I'm going to kill Danny after school. With any luck, he's kept his promise and is outside by now.

Thump!

A book lands on the carpet next to my desk. It's *The Wonderful World of Freshwater Fish*, and I have no doubt who threw it.

Another book sails over the top of the shelves and lands on my desk. Whack! Another hits the top edge of the desk and bounces off onto the student in front of me.

'Ouch!' he yells, turning to me. 'Quit it!'

I shrug.

'It wasn't me,' I say.

The books keep coming. And so does Mrs Wharton.

'Stand up!' she says. 'Would you mind telling me what's going on here?'

'Somebody is throwing books over the tops of the shelves,' I say.

'Who?'

'I don't know.'

She strides off and checks each of the aisles. Any moment now she's going to see Danny and chuck him out. Good riddance I reckon.

'I can't see anybody,' she says. 'Perhaps you'd better tell me how these books really ended up on the floor.'

I don't know what to say.

Over Mrs Wharton's shoulder I can see the A–G fiction shelf rocking back and forth. Danny's gone crazy. The excitement of thinking he's invisible has gone to his head. I've got to stop him before he goes too far.

'Excuse me, Mrs Wharton,' I say. 'Back in a minute.'

'Where do you think you're going?'

I dash to the seriously rocking shelf to try to pull Danny away and bring him to his senses, but it's already too late. The shelf tilts too far to the right. All the books fall onto the carpet. The force of the bookshelf striking the next shelf pushes it over and the combined weight of these two pushes the third shelf over. Just like a row of dominoes. Except heavier. And louder.

There is silence. Nobody can believe what they've

just seen. I turn around. Mrs Wharton is speechless. She is opening and closing her mouth like a fish.

But Danny hasn't finished yet.

He's approaching Mrs Wharton from behind, one of her prized hanging-basket ferns in his hand. The ferns that she waters so lovingly every morning before school. The ferns that if anyone so much as looks at them – let alone touches them – they cop one of Mrs Wharton's famous glares.

Danny's staring straight ahead and carrying the pot plant in his raised outstretched arms, like it's the AFL Premiership Cup.

'No!' I yell, but it's like he's possessed.

He tips it upside down over Mrs Wharton's head. Fern fronds and clumps of dirt and little white fertiliser pellets spill all over her hair, down her face and onto her yellow dress. They collect in a pile at her feet.

Danny is just standing there laughing. Poor guy. He still thinks he's invisible.

Mrs Wharton wheels around.

'Just what do you think you're doing?' she says to him.

'Who?' he says.

'You!' she says, going red in the face.

'But you can't see me,' says Danny. 'I'm invisible!'

'Invisible? Well, we'll see about that!' she says.

She reaches out, and grabs his ear and twists it at least 360 degrees – and then – judging by the expression on Danny's face – another 360 degrees after that.

Danny drops to his knees in pain.

'Oww! Oww! Let me go!' he says.

'There,' she says. 'Feeling a little more visible now?'

I must admit I'm enjoying the spectacle. After all, Danny had no qualms about getting me into trouble.

'Now,' she says, looking from Danny to me, 'both of you pack up your books, and get straight to the principal's office! And consider yourselves banned from the library for the rest of the year.'

Both of us? The rest of the year? Great. There goes my history assignment. And my English wide reading. And my social studies research. How could Danny be so dumb?

I gather up my books. There's no use arguing.

Mrs Wharton escorts us to the door and slams it behind us.

'Danny,' I say, turning to face him, 'you are a prize drongo. Did you really think . . .'

But I don't finish my question. Danny's not there.

'Dan?' Where are you?'

I hear a giggle and then a tremendous belch in my right ear. It's so loud it almost ruptures my ear-drum.

I spin around.

'Danny?'

But there's no sign of him – no visible sign anyway – jus the sound of his crazy laughter echoing down the empty corridor.

The principal can wait. I'm going straight to sick bay. I'm feeling a little faint myself.

ANDY GRIFFITHS lives in Melbourne with his family. His books include *The Day My Bum Went Psycho* and *Zombie Bums from Uranus* as well as the extremely popular *Just* series: *Just Tricking!*, *Just Annoying!*, *Just Stupid!*, *Just Crazy!* and *Just Disgusting!* The *Just* series has been adapted as a 26-episode television cartoon series called 'What's With Andy?', which screens around the world. His book *Just Disgusting!*, topped both the children's and adult bestseller lists when it was released in Australia in 2002, and *The Day my Butt Went Psycho* debuted at number eight on the *New York Times* children's bestseller list on its release in the US in April 2003. Andy's most recent books are *The Bad Book* and the final book in the *Bum* trilogy: *Bumageddon: The final pongflict*.

ZEKE AND EPPIE AND THE HEADLESS GHOST

Excerpt from *My Sister's a Nightmare*
GRETEL KILLEEN

Zeke and Eppie are trapped in their mother's ridiculous nightmare full of googly ghosts, drastic draculas, spiralling spiders, haunted houses, vampish vampires, potent potions, rapping bats and disgusting meals that never ever end. And then, along comes the Head Ghost or the headless Head of the Ghosts . . . Will Eppie and Zeke escape from the nightmare or will they be stuck in their mother's bad thoughts forever?

'Perhaps this is a joke,' howled the werewolf that was once a sunny beach. 'I mean, if these two really don't have the power to change us into things maybe they're not the wicked versions of themselves after all.'

'Indeed,' said the creaking door that used to be a double chocolate thick shake. 'There is only one way to tell if these creatures are tricking us, and that is to take them up to Skeleton Mountain. There the Head Ghost will use the full moon to take an x-ray of them and we'll be able to see straight through these two and discover what they're hiding.'

'Huuuuuuuuuuuuuuuuuuuuuuuuuugh,' said every single thing that was down in the dungeon that could make that huuuuuuuuuuuuuuuuuuuuuuuuuugh sort of noise.

'But does that mean they'll see my Barbie doll underpants?' whimpered Zeke. 'I hope so,' giggled Eppie.

And so a long procession was formed as the sad nightmare ghouls and goblins and monsters and clanging chains and howling winds and sudden bumps and shivers-up-the-spine turned Zeke and Eppie into a pair of stinking old gym shoes and then followed the two of them as they trundled up to Skeleton Mountain.

'Do you think we could call a cab?' said Eppie after a while as they turned right onto the river of earwax.

'No, I don't think they have cabs here,' said Zeke. 'I think they just have evil eels, planes that crash and insects that burrow under your skin and live there forever and ever.'

So on they marched.

'You know what my worst nightmare is?' said Eppie.

'Let me guess,' said Zeke. 'That your hair isn't brushed?'

'No, my worst nightmare is that I get up and go school one morning and forget to put my clothes on.'

'I can assure you,' said Zeke, 'that seeing you in the nude, is absolutely everyone's nightmare.'

On and on and on they walked, past their mother's most frightening nightmarish thoughts. Here they saw a train that had caught fire, there they saw a grocery bill of eight million dollars, far away they saw Neville the Nerd from the newsagency asking Mum on a date, and over there they saw their mum walking to the corner shop with the back of her dress accidentally tucked into her underpants. Oooops!

But still the weary Zeke and Eppie and their kooky, spooky companions wandered on and on and on . . . past empty milk cartons that had been put back in the fridge, public telephones that were always broken, and old ladies who bashed supermarket trolleys into the back of your ankles . . . until finally the procession arrived at the base of Skeleton Mountain.

'Oh thank heavens there's an elevator!' said Eppie happily as she looked up at the mountain with her shoe tongue hanging out.

'The elevator's broken,' said Zeke sadly.

'Arrrrrrrrrr, what a nightmare!' wailed Eppie.

And so the procession began to climb the mountain. Through the forest of the dead they wandered, past bulging eyes that had no bodies and past frightening rustles of leaves. Zeke and Eppie thought they saw things that didn't exist and they felt things they couldn't see, and . . . they smelt things that were themselves . . . stinky old gym shoes.

The wind was cold, so bitterly cold and for every step they took forward they seemed to move more than two steps back.

Finally Zeke and Eppie could go no further and stopped by their mother's second worst nightmare . . . a set of bathroom scales.

'Tell the spooky people we have to stop,' said Eppie to a scab that would never heal.

'They have to stop!' the scab told the biting wind who then carried the message up the mountain until it got tangled in a death valley and echoed and echoed in a most annoying way way way way way.

But at least the message was heard by the head of the ghosts – or the Headless Head of the Ghosts, as he was more accurately called.

'What do you mean, they're too tired to come up?' said the headless Head Ghost. 'What sort of baddies are they? Surely if they really were Dr Freckle and Miss Hide 'n' Seek they'd put on a better show of bravery than this!'

'It may be a trick,' said the bossy teacher's pet who, let's face it, is everyone's nightmare. 'I suspect the prisoners may be very evil and are desperately trying to cover it up.'

'Then I have no choice but to zoosh-fly-swoop down to them,' said the headless Head Ghost 'and see if I can see through their trickery.'

'Oh bravo,' said the bossy teacher's pet, because she was also a crawler.

Well the headless Head Ghost wanted to zoosh-fly-swoop but honestly by the time he'd ironed his official Head Ghost sheet and fastened all his medals he was running far, far, far too late to zoosh-fly-swoop. So he grabbed Skeleton Mountain's Polaroid camera, hopped on the sort of rain cloud that ruins every picnic, and poured down to the bottom of the mountain instead. Splatter splatter splatter splatter splatter. And then the ghost pulled himself together, dried himself off with a portable ghost dryer and summoned the very tired Zeke and Eppie-stinky-gym-shoes.

GRETEL KILLEEN started her career as a stand-up comic. She appears regularly on national television and radio and hosts the *Big Brother* shows. Her books include the *My Sister's* and *Very Naughty Mother* series, plus the Fleur Trotter – *My Life* – series. Gretel is currently running around like a headless chooks raising her son and daughter, preparing several of her works for TV and film, and writing an adult novel.

DO YOU WANT TO GO WITH ME?

Excerpt from *Cool School*
JOHN MARSDEN

It's your first day at your new cool school. By lunchtime you could have gone into the wrong toilets, gatecrashed the staff room, blown up the science block, been hypnotised by the principal, asked for a date, broken every bone in your body. You could have felt joy, fear, love, revenge, rage, embarrassment... You could have become your school's biggest hero... or its biggest loser... It's up to you. You make it happen.

34

That night your best friend chucks gravel at your window to wake you up. You're awake anyway, after a terrible dream about being locked for days in the wrong toilet, while teachers and students crowd around outside waiting for you to come out. When you hear the gravel you tiptoe to the window and look through. It's so late – about 11.30. What's going on?

'Having trouble with your Maths homework?' you whisper.

'No, idiot. Get some clothes on and come out here.'

You must be an idiot, because you do it. 'What do you want?' you ask, when you finally get outside.

'I'm bored. Let's go have an adventure.'

'An adventure? Now I know you're crazy. We've got school tomorrow.'

'Oh come on, don't be boring. Let's go down the cemetery.'

You're too tired to argue so you go along without any more fuss, but yawning all the way.

You get in the cemetery five minutes before midnight. It's quiet in there, too quiet. You're not tired any more, but you wish you were.

'Let's go home,' you whisper.

'Nah, what's the matter? Are you a coward?'

A church clock in the distance strikes midnight. As it finishes you see a ghostly figure appear through the wall of the graveyard. You grab your friend's arm: you're both shaking so much you're scared your teeth will fall out. Then you recognise the figure in the distance.

It's Sam Jarre!

'It's Sam Jarre!'

'I know, I know!'

Sam goes to the stone crypt in a corner of the cemetery. It's the oldest, coldest, loneliest part of the whole place. Sam seems to float over there, then disappear into the crypt. You know your hair's standing up like it's been gelled.

'I don't want to be here. Let's go play in the crocodile pond at the zoo,' you say. 'It's safer there.'

'Don't be such a wimp,' your friend replies. 'Let's check it out.'

IF YOU GO THE CRYPT, TURN TO 64.

64

You can't believe you're doing this but, after all, everyone's entitled to one mistake. You just hope you get to live long enough to make some more. The two of you tiptoe towards the crypt. The door is half open, creaking slowly in the breeze. There's a candle burning inside, and you can see a slowly moving shadow on the wall. You feel a terrible coldness that makes your skin tingle. But you can't help yourself: you've got no thoughts of going home now. You just have to know what's going on.

Slowly, ever so slowly, like you can't control it yourself, your hand rises and pushes the door wide open. Inside there's a frightening sight. It's Sam all right, opening the lid of a large old dark coffin. You and your friend stand there in shock. Sam turns and looks at you, showing no surprise at your presence.

'What . . . what are you doing?' you manage to ask.

Sam smiles at you but the smile makes you shiver even harder.

'I'm going back to where I belong.'

'But . . . but who are you?'

'You don't need to know that.'

'Where are you going?'

'I'm going to sleep again for another thousand years.'

By now Sam has the lid of the coffin open and is climbing inside.

'But . . . but only this morning you asked me if I would go with you . . .'

'Yes,' Sam says, now in the coffin and closing the lid. 'I wanted some company.' The lid is now completely closed and only a muffled voice can be heard, as if from a great distance. 'I thought you could spend the next ten centuries with me.'

The candle suddenly goes out and a sharp cold wind rushes through the crypt. You and your friend race outside screaming. You sprint all the way home and hide under the bed for the rest of the night.

In the morning you think maybe it's a dream and so you go to school to see if Sam's there. But something very strange has happened. Not only is there no Sam, but no one's ever heard of Sam. And that includes your best friends, who'd had crushes on Sam. But now it's like everyone's memory banks are completely wiped. Why, even your very best friend, who at midnight was in the cemetery with you as you grabbed each other and shook in terror together, seems to have forgotten the whole thing.

Yes, there's only one thing that makes you know for sure that Sam Jarre actually existed. It's that little scrap of paper with seven sinister words on it: 'Do you want to go with me?'

THE END

JOHN MARSDEN was born in Melbourne in 1950. He grew up in Kyneton and Devonport, and he abandoned University for a series of jobs which included collecting blood, looking after a mortuary at nights, working on a sideshow, and guarding Australia's oldest house from vandals. It was not until he was twenty-eight that he found a career that suited him – teaching. John began work as an English teacher at All Saint's College Bathurst, and then moved to Geelong Grammar School where he became Head of English at the Timbertop campus. During a three-week vacation from school John wrote a short novel that he thought might be worth publishing. Calling it *Diary* he sent it to six different publishers until the Sydney publisher, Walter McVitty Books, made an offer for it. It was published in 1987 with the new title *So Much To Tell You*. Other books written by John Marsden are: *Letters From the Inside*, *The Great Gatenby*, the best-selling *Tomorrow* series, *Dear Miffy*, *The Rabbits*, *The Boy You Bought Home*, *Millie*, *Cool School* and *Creep Street*.

30 AUSTRALIAN GHOST STORIES FOR CHILDREN

EMILY AND THE GHOST SHIP

Excerpt from *Emily Eyefinger and the Ghost Ship*
DUNCAN BALL

Emily and her parents were getting fish and chips for lunch. The shop was out on the pier over the water. They were the only people in the shop. A woman was doing the cooking.

Finally a boy at the counter called out, 'Your order is ready, folks.'

Emily went to the counter. She waited as the boy wrapped up the fish and chips in a big piece of paper. He started to hand it to Emily but stopped and said in a low voice, 'I saw the ghost ship.'

Emily was surprised. 'I beg your pardon?'

'The ghost ship. I saw it this morning. I was out fishing with my dad. It was sailing along all by itself. No one was on it. And then it disappeared.' He whispered, 'I think it's Fabian. He's back.' ...

. . . 'Do you know the story about Hannah and Fabian?'

'Yes. It's really sad.'

'It's spooky, if you ask me. I did see his ship, you know. I wasn't kidding. I was fishing in Dad's boat this morning but we had to come back because of the fog. Dad was down below getting something. Then suddenly the mist cleared and there was this big old boat with its sails all torn. I couldn't see anyone on it. I called out to Dad but the fog came in again. He doesn't believe me. Nobody believes me. I don't even know if *I* believe me.'

'Maybe you imagined it,' Emily said.

'Maybe, but I really did see something. And seeing is believing. I wasn't trying to shock you when I said I saw it.'

Emily was careful not to show Danny her eyefinger. Now *that* would be a shock.

'Sometimes there are things that we just can't explain,' Emily said. (She was thinking of eyes on fingers.)

Emily and Danny sat on the rock next to Hannah and talked and talked. When a cold wind blew, Emily took the bubble off her finger and reached back to turn up her collar. When she did, she saw something with her eyefinger. It was a dark shape out in the water.

'There's something out there,' Emily said. 'And I think it's coming our way.'

'Where?'

Emily turned around and pointed.

'You're right,' Danny said. 'There is something there. How did you see it? Do you have eyes in the back of your head or something?'

'Well, not exactly,' she said.

They watched as the shape grew bigger. The mist began to clear. There was the old ship with torn sails moving slowly towards them.

'The ghost ship,' Danny whispered. 'It's here.'

Emily watched as it came closer.

'Come on!' Danny said. 'Let's go and tell my dad.'

'No, wait,' Emily said. 'Hello! Hello! Can you hear me? Is anyone there?

There was no answer.

'Emily! Come on!'

'But we've got to get to the ship.'

'No! There's a ghost on it!'

'If there is, he's not doing a very good job of sailing,' Emily said. 'The ship is about to hit the rocks at the base of the point!'

'I think it's going to miss them,' Danny said.

'Well, then it'll go right into the harbour and hit the boats. Come on, Danny!'

Emily ran down to the rocks as the ship passed. She grabbed a rope that hung from one of the masts.

'I'm going on it!' she said. 'You have to help me!'

With this, Emily gripped the rope and swung onto the deck. She threw the rope back to Danny.

'Come on, Danny! I don't know anything about boats!'

'Oh, Emily,' Danny sighed. 'Why are we doing this?'

With a great swing, Danny landed on the deck beside her. He quickly untied a rope and let the last bit of sail down.

'We're still moving,' Emily said.

'We're drifting with the waves now,' Danny said. 'We'll have to drop anchor.'

There was a rusty metal clip that held the anchor. Danny tried to undo it but couldn't.

'It's no use,' he said. 'Let's lower the dinghy and get off this thing.'

The ship bumped against a fishing boat, pushing it out of the way. 'If this keeps up, it'll hit the pier and wreck it. Come on, let's look for a hammer or something to get the anchor loose. Where would one be?'

'I don't know, down below I guess. And I'm not going down there! It's too spooky.'

'Don't be silly,' Emily said, starting down the stairs. 'I don't see any ghosts!'

'Emily, you can't see ghosts! That's why they're called ghosts!'

It was dark on the stairs but Emily found a torch clipped to the wall. She grabbed it and turned it on. She looked all around.

'I can't find any tools or anything,' she called to Danny. 'Can you come down and help me look?'

'Okay,' Danny answered with a shaky voice.

He climbed down the stairs very slowly. At the bottom of the stairs he looked around.

'It's okay, Danny. There are no ghosts here,' Emily said. 'See, it's perfectly safe.'

'Hmm. We'll see.'

Danny found a small cabinet and opened it. Inside was a pile of tools. Danny picked up a hammer.

Just as Danny and Emily were about to start up the stairs, there was a strange noise.

'Ooooohhhhhh.'

'What was that?!' Danny whispered.

'Ooooohhhhhh.' The sound came again.

'There's someone here,' Emily said.

'And there's someone about to get out of here,' Danny said. 'Me!'

'I can hear you,' a distant voice said. 'I'm over here.'

'The ghost!' Danny said, holding up the hammer. 'Let's get out of here, Emily!'

'Come here,' the voice said.

Emily followed the sound of the voice towards the

back of the boat but there was no one there,

'I'm here,' the voice said again. '*Ooooohhhhhh.*'

'There's no one here!' Danny whispered. 'Come on!'

'No, wait.'

Emily shone her torch around the empty hold. Then she noticed two knot holes in the boards under her feet. She got down on her knees and pointed the torch down one of them. She put her face down and looked down the other.

'Anything down there?' Danny asked.

'I don't see anything, but just a minute.'

With this, Emily took the plastic bubble off her eyefinger.

'What's that?!' Danny cried. 'Oh, no!' You've got an eye on your finger!'

'Yes, I do and if you don't mind, I'm going to look down this hole with it,' Emily said. 'It comes in very handy sometimes.'

'And you said *I* was weird,' Danny said.

With her eyefinger down the hole, Emily could see a man's face looking back at her.

'Quick!' she said to Danny. 'Let's get these boards up!' Emily put the claw of the hammer between the boards. 'Help me get these up!'

Emily and Danny prised up one board and then another. Finally, they found the man, lying on his back in some cold water.

'Thank goodness,' he said. 'I climbed under the floor to patch a leak but then I got stuck. I've been down here all day. I thought I was going to die.'

'So . . . so you're not a ghost?' Danny said.

'What? No. I mean, I was sailing around the world and I got caught in a storm. Where did you kids come from? Are we near Rocky Crag?'

'We certainly are! Oh, no! The anchor!' Danny yelled, racing up the stairs.

Emily could hear Danny banging away up above. Then she heard the sound of the anchor splashing into the water. When Emily and the man got up to the deck, the boat was only metres from Danny's fish pier.

'Hey, that was a close call,' the man said. 'If it hadn't been for you kids, my boat would have been wrecked and I'd have been drowned. How did you see me down under the deck?'

'With this,' Emily said, holding up her eyefinger.

'Goodness me! An eye on a finger! I don't believe it!'

'Well, seeing is believing,' Emily said with a laugh.

And Danny and the lone sailor gave a big laugh too.

DUNCAN BALL was born in the United States and then moved around a lot with his family before coming to Sydney in 1974. He began work as an industrial chemist but he soon decided he wanted to fulfil his original dream of becoming a writer and began writing for both adults and children. Duncan is best known as the creator of the *Selby the Talking Dog* series, beginning with *Selby's Secret*. His other books include the *Emily Eyefinger* series, the *Ghost of the Gory* series and a number of books in the *Case Of* series. Duncan lives in Glebe with his wife and their cat, Jasper.

TASHI AND THE GHOSTS

From *The Big, Big, Big Book of Tashi*
ANNA FIENBERG AND
BARBARA FIENBERG

'Guess what Tashi is having for dinner tonight,' said Jack, as he spooned up the last strawberry.

'Roast leg of lion caught fresh from the jungle,' Jack's father said keenly.

'Wrong!' Jack laughed.

'Grilled tail of snake caught fresh from the desert,' his mother said proudly.

'Double wrong! He's having Ghost Pie, from a special recipe that he learned from –'

'Ghosts!' cried Mum and Dad together.

'Right!' said Jack. 'And would you like to know how he came by this spooky recipe?'

'Yes indeed,' said Mum.

'Can't wait,' said Dad, getting comfortable on the sofa. 'So tell us. After Tashi tricked those giants and teased the bandits, how did he meet these *ghosts*?'

'Well, it was like this,' said Jack. 'The very night that Tashi escaped from the bandits' camp and ran home to his village, Third Uncle saw a ghost light shining in the forest.'

'What does a ghost light look like? How would I know if I saw one?' asked Mum nervously.

'Like a street lamp, without the post?' guessed Dad.

Jack shook his head. 'No, Tashi said it was more like a small moon, sending out rays of light into the trees, like white spider threads.'

'Ooh, can you get tangled up in them?' shivered Mum.

'In a way,' said Jack. 'Ghost monsters can be sticky, and they tend to hang around, Tashi says. Well, the next night there were more ghost lights. They came closer, and closer, and Tashi called his parents to see. Soon the news spread through the village and everyone was peeping behind their curtains at the phantom lights flitting through the forest.

'In the morning the people hurried to the square to talk about the ghosts. Some wanted to pack their belongings and move right away. Others wanted to burn down the forest so the ghosts would have no place to live. Finally they decided to ask Wise-As-An-Owl what he thought would be the best plan.'

'My plan would be to ignore them,' said Dad. 'If the ghosts got no attention, they'd probably go away.'

'I don't think that works with ghosts, Dad,' said Jack. 'Anyway, Wise-As-An-Owl told the men to organise a great beating of saucepan lids outside their houses that night as soon as it grew dark. They did, and sure enough, the ghosts slipped away, back into the forest.

'But the next night the ghosts came back. They drifted up like smoke, nearer and nearer, until they were pressing their faces against the widows. Their mouths were huge and gluey, and the air in the houses began to grow stale and thin as they sucked at the keyholes and under the doors.

Everybody in the village burst out into the streets, coughing and choking. Men and women thundered around making a great crashing noise with saucepans and garbage lids and firecrackers. The ghosts melted away but Tashi was sure that they weren't gone for long.'

'They'd have gone forever if people had ignored them,' muttered Dad. 'Who comes back for no attention?'

'Well,' continued Jack, 'in the morning Tashi went to see his father's Younger Brother. He lives up on a hill overlooking the village and spends his nights studying the stars through a great telescope that he built years ago.

'Tashi told him about the ghost monsters who were frightening the villagers and he cried, "Of course, I know why they have come now. Look, Tashi," and he took out his charts of the stars and his Book of Calculations. "You see, look here. In three days' time there will be an eclipse of the moon."'

'I'll bet Tashi didn't know what *that* was,' Dad laughed. He was already looking for the dictionary.

'Yes, said Jack patiently. 'It's what happens when the moon is blacked out for a while by the shadow of the earth. Well, Younger Brother said to Tashi, "Last time there was an eclipse, the river flooded and your father's pigs were drowned. And the time before that we had a plague of locusts that ate the village fields bare. You'll see, with this next eclipse there will be a haunting of ghosts."

'At that, Tashi thought "*Aha!*", and he began to form one of his cunning plans. He waited two more days and sure enough the saucepan lids did no good at all. Each night after the people went to bed, the ghosts floated back to the village. On the third night, a brave dog rushed out of his house but as he drew his breath to bark, he sucked in a tendril of grey ghost, and it was terrible to see. He choked and gasped and his fine black coat grew pale and wispy until he was just a shadow, melting into the stones.

'The villagers drew their curtains against the sight of it, but Tashi crept into the forest. At first he could see only the small moons of light, tangling amongst the leaves. But as he tip-toed into the dark heart of the forest, he saw the ghosts themselves.

'And there were hundreds of them – hopping ghosts, prowling ghosts, gliding ghosts. They were like white dripping shadows, fat and thin, tall and tiny, whipping all around him.

'Suddenly Tashi felt a cold weight on his head. "Oh no, a jumping ghost," he thought, and he tried to pull it off. But it slid down over his eyes and nose like sticky egg white, and he could hardly see or breathe. "Oh no, a jumping *and* slithering ghost," he groaned, as it trickled down his back and clamped his arms.

'"Let me go!" Tashi screamed, and as he screamed he sucked in a bit of cold eggy ghost. He felt as if he were choking, and then more and more ghosts pressed their bodies against him. Like thickening fog they crowded around and Tashi didn't want to breathe for fear of sucking in those damp whirling phantoms.

'And then a huge glowing ghost as big as a ship loomed over him. Its eyes were empty, and it was the meanest-looking ghost Tashi had ever seen.'

'Has Tashi seen many ghosts before this?' asked Dad.

'Yes, he's seen a few in his time, he says. Well, this mean-looking, leader ghost asked Tashi why he had come into the forest at night.

'"I've come to warn you," Tashi hissed at him,

blowing out wisps of ghost as he spoke. "If you don't leave our village at once, you will all suffer."

'The huge ghost laughed. The sound rippled like wind through the forest. "And how exactly will we suffer?"

'"Well," Tashi told him, "my friend the Red-Whiskered Dragon-Ghost will come and punish you if you hurt me or frighten the people in my village."

'There was a low buzz as the ghosts swarmed together, discussing Tashi's news. The smaller ghosts were trembling, and their outlines were fading a little with fear. But the leader ghost was scornful. "Why should we believe *you*? No one could hurt *us*!"

'"Oh, I can easily prove it," Tashi said. "Just look at the moon up there. See how round and full it is? Now I will call my friend, the Red-Whiskered Dragon-Ghost, and he will open his huge jaws and eat the moon right up. When the moonlight disappears you will know how great he is and you will be afraid."

'Tashi called out into the night, "Oh mighty Red-Whiskered Dragon-Ghost, when I count to three, please open your jaws and take your first gigantic bite out of the moon!"

'Tashi counted *o-n-e* very, very slowly. He was worrying, deep inside himself – what if Younger Brother was wrong with his calculations? Could an eclipse be late?

'He counted *t-w-o* even more slowly. Was the moon shrinking a little?

'"Are you ready, ghost monsters?" Tashi cried, and then he shouted, "*THREE!*" just as the black shadow of the earth moved across the moon and sliced off a great piece.

'The ghosts watched as the moon grew smaller and

smaller until there was not even a needlepoint of light in the dark sky. The moon had been swallowed up.

'The ghosts moaned with fear and their sighs blew through the trees like a gale of ice. "Please," they cried to Tashi, "tell your friend to give us back the moon. Tell him to spit it out again!"

'Tashi was silent for a moment, letting the ghosts feel the awful weight of a sky without light. Their own little moons of ghost-light were paler now, swamped by the darkness of the night.

'"All right," Tashi said finally, "I will ask him to grant you your wish – if you do two things. First, you must all leave this part of the earth, and never come back. Every now and again, the Red-Whiskered Dragon-Ghost will gobble up the moon for a short time, just to remind you never to frighten my village and its people again."

'"Very well," the leader ghost grudgingly agreed. "And the second thing?"

'"You must give me the recipe for Ghost Pie. I have heard that it is delicious, and for three days after eating it a person can walk through solid walls."

'The ghost leader let out a roar of rage. The little ghosts quivered and faded into the trees. They were shrinking with every moment, hanging like cloudy raindrops from the forest leaves.

'"Ghost Pie is one of our greatest secrets," the leader ghost spat. He waved for some of the older ghosts to come closer. They whispered together and then the leader ghost turned to Tashi. "We will do as you say, young Tashi, if you promise never to reveal the ingredients to any other *living* soul."'

'Aha!' cried Dad, slapping his knee. 'So when are we going to have a taste of pie?'

'Tashi says we can all come over to dinner next

Saturday to try it, as long as we don't ask any questions about how it is made,' said Jack.

'It's a promise,' beamed Dad. He stood up and stretched. 'Oh well,' he said, 'I suppose that's the end of the story, and Tashi's had no more trouble with ghosts then.'

'That's right,' smiled Jack, 'but only one moon went by before he was in a sticky situation with a truly wicked Baron!'

ANNA FIENBERG is a storyteller much loved for her works of fantasy and magic. She grew up in a house filled with books and started writing stories when she was eight, but never imagined being an author. She studied psychology, fascinated by the dark world of dreams. She gave up counselling after an unfortunate incident with an enraged man and a chair, began writing and scored a job working for *School Magazine*. As an editor she also had to write reviews and articles, stories and plays, as well as reading over a thousand books a year. One of the stories she wrote for *School Magazine* later became her first book. In partnership with her mother, **BARBARA FIENBERG** who used to be a teacher librarian, she creates the tall stories loved by children when they enter the world of Tashi. Anna also has an ongoing creative partnership with the illustrator Kim Gamble to produce such books as *The Magnificent Nose and Other Marvels*, *The Hottest Boy Who Ever Lived*, the *Tashi* series, the *Minton* picture books, and *Joseph*.

TRAPPED!

Excerpt from *Murder on the Ghoul Bus*
MARGARET CLARK

Every day it's the same routine: the same bus stop, same friends, same cranky old bus driver Mr Dumbleton. But when Mr Dumbleton collapses across the steering wheel one Monday morning, everything changes. Suddenly, there's a new driver and the ride to school will never be boring again!

Everyone stared in horror as he got on the bus.

'Hmm,' Mr Dumbleton said to the driver. 'It's nice and warm in here. All these sweaty little bodies. I forgot how lovely and cosy it is in the school bus, eh.'

He turned to face them. They gasped.

He had no eyes! Maggots had already started eating him. Several wriggled round in his eye sockets then dropped, squirming, onto the floor. One wriggled up his left nostril. He was covered with bits of dirt and his skin was blue and wrinkled.

'They put me in a cheap cardboard coffin,' he

explained to the terrified passengers. 'The maggots got in straight away. Imagine: you live a healthy life, good fresh food, an apple a day and no junk stuff, eight hours' sleep with the bedroom window up for fresh air; you get immunised, checked over by doctors, and finally you keel over, die, and become maggot fodder. But at least these maggots are getting a healthy meal off me!'

He picked the maggot out of his nose and swallowed it.

'Might as well get an inside start,' he wheezed. 'But they seem to go for the eyes first. Prefer the jelly, I suppose. And the brain. They're keen on brain food. There's about fifty wriggling round in my head sampling my long term memory. It sort of tickles a bit. But I can still think, eh. And I don't need my eyes to see.'

As they all stared in horror his eye sockets began to glow with a luminous green light.

'Enough for now,' said the corpse of Mr Dumbleton. 'We have to get going. We have a drive ahead of us.'

Tom found his voice.

'But you – you're supposed to be *dead*.'

'Of course I'm dead, boy. That is, dead in *your* terms. Do you find this strange?'

'Well – er – to be honest, yes. You're supposed to be lying at rest in your coffin, not jaunting about the countryside,' said Tom, bravely meeting the glowing green eyes with a steady stare. 'And can you tell the driver he's gone the wrong way? We're supposed to be going to school.'

The driver and the corpse of Mr Dumbleton looked at each other. Then they both threw back their heads and started cackling away like they were going to lay eggs.

'Going to school? On the school bus? Ha ha ha, that's a laugh!' grinned the driver.

'Well, they *are* going to school in a manner of speaking,' said the corpse of Mr Dumbleton, and he rocked back and forward with mirth, wiping the green slime that oozed from his eye sockets. He turned round.

'Yes, you are going to school. You've just graduated to Higher Education. Aren't you lucky? You passed "GO", but you're not collecting two hundred dollars!'

He cackled away to himself.

'What's he raving on about?' whispered Alice. 'Or are we all having a terrible nightmare?'

'We're not dreaming. This is for real,' said Harry. 'And I think he's playing Monopoly in his head. You know, pass GO and collect two hundred dollars.'

'What's he mean by Higher Education?' said Cathy as the driver and the corpse muttered to each other, horrible heads close together. 'I thought we *were* having Higher Education. We're at high school, aren't we?'

'I think this is all a huge practical joke,' said Tom as the bus rumbled to life. 'Someone's trying to scare us. It's time for a showdown.'

He stood up and turned to face everyone.

'Okay, you've had your fun,' he said. 'You all acted like you were zombies when you got on the bus. And now you've somehow managed to re-create a Dumbo look-alike from the grave. Very clever. But we're tired of all this. The joke's over. Can we go to school now?'

But the bus was silent. The other kids sat straight and still, staring straight ahead, except for Cathy, Alice and Harry, who were starting to look *really* scared.

'They're doing it again,' said Cathy in a trembling voice. 'They're pretending to be like zombies.'

Alice pinched Kate. Really hard. She didn't even flinch.

'They're all in some sort of trance again.'

'Why?' asked Harry. 'And how come *we're* not?'

'I dunno. But I'm going to find out, and there's only one way to do it.'

Tom stood up. He marched up the aisle, leant over the driver and yanked the keys out of the ignition. The fog was lifting. They'd reached the cemetery. All around were tombstones and graves of the dead neatly laid out in rows like fish on marble slabs. Everything looked cold, grey and spooky in the swirling mist. Then the sun came out, breaking through the fog and gleaming on the granite headstones with their faded writing. It was the land of the dead, somber and grim.

Beyond the gloomy cemetery in stark contrast was the open countryside. Just then the sun pierced through the mist to shine on green paddocks with cows contentedly munching grass. Life beyond death.

Tom slid back the nearest window and pitched the keys as far as he could. They fell with a dull clunk on the nearest grave and slid down out of sight into the long grass near the headstone.

'Now,' he said. 'Let us out. *We* prefer to walk!'

'You shouldn't have done that, boy,' said the driver with an evil leer. 'Because of your foolish act we're going to be late.'

'Well, bad luck,' said Tom. 'Come on, gang.'

He stood at the top of the steps as Harry, Cathy and Alice walked up the aisle to the front of the bus.

'Hey. All of you. Come *on*!' he called to the others.

But the other kids sat still and lifeless in their seats, staring straight ahead.

'Unzap them,' said Tom to the driver. 'We're out of here. All of us. And open the door. *Now.*'

'You ain't going nowhere,' said the driver in a cold, steely voice.

MARGARET CLARK was born in 1945 and has worked as a teacher, a university lecturer and at the Geelong Centre for Alcohol and Drug Dependency before writing full-time. Her novels for older readers include *The Big Chocolate Bar*, *Fat Chance*, *Hot or What*, *Kiss and Make Up*, *Famous for Five Minutes* and a trilogy about the Studley family: *Hold My Hand or Else!*, *Living with Leanne* and *Pulling the Moves*. Her *Secret Girls' Stuff*, *More Secret Girls' Stuff*, and *What to do When Life Sucks* have become best-sellers.

LIAR GHOST

7

GOLDIE ALEXANDER

All year Kian's class had been looking forward to their trip to the desert.

But when he climbed onto the bus, Damon pointed to the drizzle outside. 'Bet it keeps on raining.'

'No way,' said Van. 'It hardly ever rains in the desert.'

As the bus drove out of the city, it kept on raining. Soon the windows were too misty to see through.

The bus stopped at sunset to set up camp. The boys took ages to put up their tent. Mr Gladstone said, 'Tomorrow night less mucking around. Right?'

'Right,' they said.

The next two days it never stopped raining. Not even in the desert. The fourth day their bus broke down. A kilometre back, they'd passed an empty house. Ms Pavos said, 'That's where we'll camp tonight.'

Soon as they got inside, Damon yelled, 'This house feels haunted.'

The kids looked around. All they could see were rotten floors and damp walls.

While the boys played football with some empty cans. Damon went off to explore. He came back saying, 'Maybe this was a hotel. There's another room with a cellar.'

Down one end of that room were two small doors in the floor. 'Drover's' was carved into one. 'Arms' on the other. The letters were woven into a curious pattern. When Kian stared long enough, he saw crocodiles, spiders. Even snakes.

Damon clattered his teeth. 'Bet there's a ghost down there.'

Ms Pavos gave a dry little laugh. 'Probably ants. You're to leave those doors alone. Do you hear?'

Everyone nodded.

Around midnight, Kian woke to an unexpected hush. It took him ages to realise that the rain had stopped.

He went back to sleep. But two hours later, Damon shook him awake. 'I hear footsteps.'

'Possums!' Kian closed his eyes and rolled onto his side.

But Damon lay there listening. More like it was rats. Rats reminded him of bats. And bats of vampires. And vampires of ghosts. Now he was scared enough to wake Van.

The boys crept down the passage. The moon shone through a hole in the roof and threw shadows on the walls. The wind whistled. A door creaked open.

'What's that?'

Damon's legs felt weak. He knew that the only doors in this building led to the cellar. Just as the boys reached the end of the passage, a man with a long white beard appeared. Water streamed from his hat. It dribbled down his coat to make a puddle around his feet.

Damon guessed this was a ghost. He felt faint. He told himself to wriggle his toes and some feeling came back into his legs.

That ghost was sooo sad. Tears hung from his nose and rolled down his cheeks. His feet were ankle deep in puddles. When he opened his mouth to speak, muddy water spurted out. He said, 'Do you want to hear my story?'

The boys quickly nodded.

'Fine,' said the ghost. 'Only you mustn't interrupt.'

'Back in 1899,' he began, 'I was apprenticed to a cabinet-maker. After he died, I rode into the desert. Back then, the locals were farmers. I didn't much like farming, so I built this hotel. When a drought set in I visited a rainmaker. "I will help you find rain," the rainmaker said, "if you give me half your profits."

'I agreed. Two days later it began to rain. Soon the creeks were full and the farmers spent lots of money. But mightn't it have rained without the rainmaker's help? So I hid my money, drew a map of where it was, then told him I'd lost everything.'

'You mean,' said Van, 'you lied?'

'Yes.' More tears trickled down the ghost's face. 'The rainmaker did another dance. This time there were terrible floods and the farmers went broke . . .'

'How come,' Damon interrupted, 'that rainmaker knew you were lying?'

'Told you not to butt in!' The ghost disappeared in a clap of thunder.

Van nearly fainted. But Damon realised that if only he could find that treasure, he'd be rich. Thinking this, he scuttled back to his bag and went straight to sleep.

First thing next morning, Damon told Kian about the ghost.

Kian said, 'How do you know the treasure is here?'

'Why would the ghost lie?'

'Didn't he say he was liar?'

Damon looked uncertain. Kian glanced at Van. Van shrugged and looked away.

The boys waited for their camp to pack up. Then they crept into the room with the cellar and looked carefully around. Only bare walls and broken floorboards. They wandered outside. Just bare earth, scrubby water-laden trees, and puddles.

Where was that treasure?

Van said, 'We're leaving pretty soon. Didn't the ghost say he'd worked for a cabinet-maker?'

'That's right,' said Kian. 'Maybe that map is the pattern on the cellar doors? Damon, you stencil it off. I'll keep Mr Gladstone away.'

'I'll keep the driver busy,' Van cried.

Kian found Mr Gladstone folding tents. 'Please sir,' he cried. 'Let me do that.'

Meanwhile Damon had found a pencil and paper and crept back to the cellar. He started tracing off the pattern.

A shadow fell on him. 'Look!' Damon whispered. 'This is the map. Now we have to get inside the cellar.'

Kian said, 'But we're leaving in an hour.'

'Help me open these doors. I need something sharp.'

Kian handed over his precious pen-knife.

Once the doors were open, Damon shone his torch inside. All the boys saw were dusty walls covered in cobwebs.

Creatures scuttled across the floor.

'What's that?'

'Spiders! That's how he kept his money safe.'

'What's that on the floor?'

'Looks like old clothes,' Kian whispered. 'Someone has to climb down and see what's in there.'

Damon gulped and nodded. He knew he was that 'someone'.

Meanwhile their driver was trying to fix the bus. Van sidled over to watch. 'Can I help?'

Before he could, someone yelled, 'Look at Damon!'

Almost unrecognisable under dirt and spider webs, Damon was holding out a wooden box. It took him ages to open the lid. But when he finally did, he just managed not to cry.

That ghost turned out to be a terrible liar. Inside the box, there was nothing but old newspapers with a very detailed description of the 1899 flood.

GOLDIE ALEXANDER was born in Melbourne and went to MacRobertson Girls High. Maybe if Goldie had paid more attention to maths and science, she might have found a way seeing into the future or even invented a lighter-than-air machine. Instead, she creates stories for children of all ages. Goldie wrote her first four books under the pseudonym of Gerri Lapin. She was a co-winner in the 2000 and 2001 Mary Grant Bruce Award for two long short stories, and has written twenty-five books for adults and children, plus numerous articles and short stories. She lectures and conducts Creative Writing Workshops.

ALISTAIR

JENNY BLACKFORD

After a particularly hard day at school – my best friend Kylie still wasn't talking to me – I opened the front door, ready to be jumped on and barked at, but the corridor was quiet. Alistair just sat in polite silence on Grandpa's old blue recliner in the living room.

'Hello, boy', I said. 'Dinner?'

He woofed quietly and followed me into the kitchen. It wasn't natural, but what is these days? Especially since Grandpa was hit by a truck on his way to the health food shop, and Grandma sold their big old house and moved away.

Alistair ate his dinner with surprising delicacy, then walked sedately back to the old recliner. I fed the three goldfish that Grandma had given me for Christmas – fat golden Oscar Wilde, the fantail, and Merry and Pippin, a pair of velvety-skinned blue-grey Orandas. Then I sat down to watch TV until Mum came home from the library where she works. Not that she looks like a librarian, especially a librarian on an American sitcom. Mum's your inner-urban grunge type: spiky black hair; studded boots; and a python tattoo around her upper right arm.

Next afternoon, Alistair was quiet and polite again. I fed him, and moved on to the fish. There was poor Oscar, as fat and golden in death as he had been in life, floating at the top of the tall, hexagonal glass tank.

Quickly, before Mum got home, I scooped Oscar's corpse into the fishtank water-jug, using the little green fish-net, and buried him under the apple tree that Dad had planted in our tiny backyard. With any luck, I thought, it would be weeks before Mum noticed he was gone. She was so upset about Grandpa, and Oscar might be the last straw.

The early news was on the TV, when I got home the next afternoon. Alistair was sitting in Grandpa's old blue chair, as usual, but he wasn't dozing – he seemed to be staring at the screen.

Weird, I thought. I changed the channel to music videos.

Alistair growled. Very gently, but definitely.

'Alistair?'

He put his head on one side, gazed at me with the pleading expression that Labradors do so well and looked back at the TV.

'You want the news?' I said.

He kept looking at the TV.

I changed the channel back to the news, and fed the fish. Alistair watched the news, then looked at me and woofed quietly.

'Dinner time, now, do you think, Alistair?'

It was getting just like living with Grandpa.

The next Wednesday night, when I got up in the night to get a glass of water, I saw a fat golden shape moving in the corner of the living room. I squinted hard at it, but it didn't disappear. I walked closer, past Alistair on Grandpa's old recliner. I didn't feel cold all over, and the hairs on the back of my neck didn't bristle with terror, but it was definitely the ghost of Oscar the goldfish, swimming in air over the tall fishtank.

'Oscar, you're dead. I buried you under the apple tree.'

He took no notice, and just kept swimming big circles in the air. Merry and Pippin were playing hide-and-seek in the waterweed, as usual. Alistair wagged his tail gently. So much for animals' sixth sense.

What if Mum got up in the night, and found the ghost of Oscar the goldfish floating over his tank? Or if she came home to find Alistair in Grandpa's chair, watching the news?

On the weekend, while Mum was sleeping in, I was getting Alistair's doggy crunchies out of the cupboard, when he started whining and grabbing at my hand. 'OK, boy, what is it?' I asked, not expecting a very sensible answer. He pointed with his nose at the muesli container on the bench.

'That stuff might be people food, Alistair, but it really isn't any nicer than your crunchies. I only eat it because Grandpa told me I had to. I wouldn't eat it, if it was just up to me.'

He whined again. I tipped the muesli from my breakfast bowl into his doggy bowl, and made myself toast and honey instead.

After Alistair inhaled the bowl of muesli, he looked

disapprovingly at the last bite of toast in my hand. I just smiled. 'It *is* wholemeal bread,' I said, 'and everyone knows that honey is a health food.'

***

The game is up. Mum got home early last night, and I was sitting on the floor next to Alistair's recliner, watching the news with him. We had the newspaper spread out on the floor, and we were sharing a packet of oatmeal biscuits.

'Er, Mum . . .'

'It's OK, sweetie, I know. I watch the news with him, too, after you go to bed. And I've been giving him bran and linseed for breakfast.'

I felt my shoulders loosen up a bit, but then Mum glanced in the direction of the fish tank.

'There's something else,' she said. 'It's about Oscar . . .'

My heart sank. 'Oh, Mum, he died a few weeks ago. I should have told you, but I didn't want to upset you.'

'I guessed that, Sonya. But have you seen anything odd at night?'

Oh-oh. 'Er, something . . . floating?'

'Yup! That's what I mean. Oscar, swimming in mid-air. I'm glad you've seen him, too.' Mum gave a slightly wicked grin. 'Don't worry, sweetie, it's all fine. Oscar makes a great ghost.'

I laughed with relief. 'Actually, I thought he looked pretty good, for a dead goldfish.' It was time to take a big risk. 'And I'd missed Grandpa.'

'Yeah,' Mum said, 'I know.' She sat down on the floor, getting comfortable between us as I passed her one of the biscuits. She put her free arm around Alistair. 'I'd missed him too.'

JENNY BLACKFORD was born in Sydney and was educated in Newcastle. She now lives in a slightly spooky 1890s terrace house in Melbourne with an indoor fish-pond. In a previous life, she worked as a computer consultant on large networks in the US, Singapore and even exotic Tasmania. Nowadays, she reviews fiction for newspapers and magazines including *The Age* (the quality broadsheet in Melbourne) and *The New York Review of Science Fiction*. She also assesses manuscripts for Driftwood Manuscripts and for Penguin Australia and she has had a number of short stories published. Her science fiction story *Dave's Diary* received an honourable mention from the judges of the Children's Division of the 2003 Aurealis Awards. She prefers writing about goldfish and ghosts.

TAD DROWNS AGAIN

Excerpt from *Ghost Boy*
FELICITY PULMAN

Froggy and Cassie meet up with Tad, a young boy who drowned in mysterious circumstances in 1881. Tad died trying to protect the 'family treasure'. If his ghost can't find what has been hidden for over a hundred years, will Froggy have the courage to take Tad's place?

The two boys scowled at each other.

'Maybe you can fight about it later.' Cassie had heard enough of the conversation to work out what was going on. 'Isn't it more important now to try to get the treasure?' She glanced from Froggy to where she thought Tad might be.

Froggy shrugged. 'Cassie's right. Let's get going.' He snatched the knife from Tad's hand, closed it up and thrust it into his pocket, feeling shaky and sweaty with fear as he scrambled down the rocks after Tad. The roar of the sucking waves sounded frighteningly loud.

'You'll save me if I get into trouble then?' Tad still sounded hostile as he stepped cautiously to the edge of the ledge.

'I already told you I would. I don't break my promises,' Froggy snapped.

'You'd better not!' Tad eased himself over the ledge and into the water. He lashed out, swimming strongly, his head bobbing dark against the foam-laced water.

'Has he gone yet?' Cassie whispered.

Froggy nodded. 'Yes. He's going into the cave now.'

He sat down on the rock, pulling Cassie down beside him . . . and waited.

Nothing happened for quite some time. Then, squinting against the glare of the water, Froggy saw Tad emerge from the cave, empty-handed.

'Where's the treasure?' he shouted, jumping to his feet. But Tad didn't seem to hear him as he waded back into the water.

Froggy felt a moment of paralysing fear. 'Tad!' he shouted. 'Don't swim back!' But his words were lost in the roar of the water. He felt sick as he saw Tad lash out, trying to swim against the waves, which rose up, forcing him back into the cave.

'Is he coming? Why isn't he here yet?' asked Cassie.

'I think he's in trouble.' Froggy's teeth were clenched, all his attention strained on the sleek black head that suddenly surfaced as Tad struggled towards them.

'Tad! Hold onto me!' Froggy leaned forward, felt Cassie clasp him round the waist for balance. He leaned further. But Tad seemed not to see his outstretched arm. He was gasping for breath, fighting the ocean with all his strength, his arms flailing wildly as he went under again.

'Tad!' Froggy screamed. He shivered violently, felt the water closing over him, dragging him down. 'Tad!' he gasped as Cassie's clutching hands pulled him back from the edge.

'Don't, Cassie! Let me go!' He braced himself against

her, leant forward once more and saw Tad's drowning eyes looking into his.

'Mama.' He heard the faint sigh and found that he was looking down into an empty, churning sea.

Tad had gone. Only Cassie was left and she was shaking him violently, almost in tears. 'What's happened? My God, Froggy, you nearly went off the edge then!'

Froggy blinked at her. 'Tad's drowned,' he said.

'We already know that,' Cassie said impatiently.

'No. I mean he's drowned all over again. That's why he didn't want to go back, Cassie, don't you see? He knew what was going to happen.' Froggy hugged himself, shivering violently. 'Tad's gone.'

'Maybe he can only replay what's happened to him before.' Cassie patted Froggy's shoulder, trying to comfort him. 'But he'll come back. He always has before.'

'If he doesn't, I'm in trouble.'

'Why?'

'It means if we want the treasure, I'll have to swim out to the cave.' Froggy felt the hair prickle up the back of his neck, felt shivers run down his spine. 'I can't do it,' he said.

'You certainly can't if Tad's not here to show you where to find it.' Cassie's tone was determinedly cheerful as she continued: 'But it may not be necessary, Froggy. We've already found out heaps of stuff. I reckon we should take what we know to the authorities, those lawyer people. Let's tell them everything we've found out. They can do the rest. The treasure will still belong to you.'

But the treasure didn't seem so important to Froggy any more. 'I wish Tad would come back,' he muttered, looking around. 'I mean, he only went in because I told him that we'd save him if he got into trouble.' He stared bleakly at Cassie. 'We let him down. *I* let him down. I broke my promise, Cassie.'

'But you did your best. I know how hard you tried.' Cassie put a hand on his arm. 'Don't worry about him, Froggy. He'll come back when he wants to, you'll see.'

'I dunno.' Froggy shook his head sadly as he slowly led the way up the rocky path until they reached the ledge where Tad had met them before.

No one was there. They sat down to wait for Tad, waited until the shadows had taken all the colour from the earth and the air was chill. But there was no sign of Tad at all.

Froggy was surprised how much he missed him.

Sydney author **FELICITY PULMAN** has a passion for history and for stories of the past. Among the subjects close to her heart are the stories of the Quarantine Station close to her home and of the people who came there during Australia's early settlement. She is also intrigued by the court of the legendary King Arthur and has written short stories and three novels, *Shalott*, *Return to Shalott* and *Shalott: the Final Journey*, celebrating the romance of Arthur's court. All her books are based on meticulous research, which has included following the Arthurian trail and visiting well-known sites in both Britain and France.

PUCK GOES HOME

Excerpt from *A Ghost of a Chance*
NETTE HILTON

Anne-Marie loves her dog Maudie. To leave her behind in Australia when she goes to England for a year is about as much as she can bear. But Anne-Marie soon becomes caught up in the story of another girl, many centuries ago, who misses her beloved dog – a mysterious white ghost dog who beckons to Anne-Marie, asking her for help . . .

The wind was waiting for Anne-Marie out in the churchyard and it pulled and pressed at her track top and sneaked its mean, cold fingers around her throat.

She shivered hard now. Her teeth made little chattering noises.

She was sure she'd have to take her anorak back so she could hug parts that weren't too muddy around her. She tugged at it gently and was pleased when the small dog moved closer. He seemed to be sniffing, his nose lifted high into the wind.

Anne-Marie smelt it then, too. The sweet, stronger

smell of lavender. Only this time it was mixed with other smells that were perhaps petticoats and dresses and the soap smell that was always left when hair was washed and clean.

The misty little dog ran towards the church, lifting his paw every now and then and turning to make funny barking, yapping noises as if to tell Anne-Marie to hurry, to come with him to the door.

Anne-Marie ran behind, hugging her anorak on as she went and ignoring the big muddy splotch that was the hood.

The dog was pawing at the door now and Anne-Marie pressed behind him, leaning hard against the old, oak timbers to try and make it open. The wind whipped around them and she felt the lump come back to her throat. Sad whining sounds reached up from the misty little dog at her feet and she felt big, hot tears trickle onto her cheeks.

To get this far, so close . . .

She banged her hands hard now onto the church door and the air around them filled with perfume. Even the wind seemed to help, pressing its breath against the heavy timber and the church wall.

More than anything Anne-Marie wanted that great, heavy door to open.

Her hands hurt, a stinging hurt from beating so hard, and her fingers throbbed from the cold so that she had to stop for a minute. The dog was quiet too. And still. There was only the sound of the wind and even that seemed to settle for a second to let a new sound reach her.

Voices.

Coming closer.

Puck huddled into the darkest shadow and Anne-Marie stepped in front of him. She scrubbed the tears from her face and turned around.

'I told you she'd be here!' Edward. Good old, wonderful old Edward. He stood pointing at her from the bottom of the churchyard. 'See! I told you!' He ran over to Anne-Marie. 'What were you *doing*? I called and called and you didn't answer and I thought you'd probably fallen down the steps or something.' He was looking at her knees as if he expected to see scrapes and bruises. 'Did you hurt yourself much?'

Other people were running to her now.

'I couldn't get out,' she said. It was nearly the truth and, if he hadn't seen the white mist that hovered between her legs, well . . . it would be just too hard to explain right now. 'I thought you were mad at me.'

Edward's mum got there first. 'I rang your mother straight away, Anne-Marie. Edward was in such a state. I thought the house must have fallen in on top of you.' She gave Edward a hug.

Edward squeezed himself free. 'Get off it, Mum.' He shook his anorak back into place.

'I'm freezing.' Anne-Marie shivered great shuddery shivers. 'I had to come here,' she said. 'See, there's this statue in there . . .' Where to begin . . . where to start to try to explain.

Anne-Marie's dad arrived next and then poor Father Tom who looked like an enormous caped wonder as the wind tore his cassock.

'We were so worried!'

'Where have you been?'

'What are you doing here?'

They all asked at once and she felt herself being wrapped in scarves and hoods and a woollen beanie and her father's hands rubbing and rubbing and deliciously warming her. Nobody slowed down enough to let her answer any of their questions.

And under it all, at the back of her legs, she could feel the cold misty shape of Puck huddling harder against the wall.

'Let's get out of the wind.' Father Tom pulled an enormous key from his pocket and turned it in the lock on the door.

The dark, empty stillness of the church was refrigerator-cold as Anne-Marie stepped through following the scampering, bounding bundle of mist that ran ahead of her.

Puck raced up the centre aisle, his sore leg forgotten as he leapt onto a pew and along it. Father Tom had clicked on the lights and they made such a mixture of light and dark and jewelled brightness that a small lighter-than-light foggy mist was easily overlooked.

Anne-Marie watched as Puck crossed into the darkened corner of the chapel and made one final leap to sit at Lady Jane's feet. He turned and looked back to Anne-Marie, his paw lifted, and she saw, she *knew* she saw, the biggest doggy smile she'd ever seen in her whole life.

The air filled, in a sudden rush, with the perfumes of all the field flowers, of roses and lavender and nodding violets and the forest smell of wild thyme.

And then Puck was gone.

Only Edward spoke. 'Did someone put some flowers in here or something?' he said.

Edward hadn't left her back there in the manor house. He hadn't just run off – he'd gone to get help.

Anne-Marie laughed. A wonderful laugh that bubbled right down from the deep in her tummy. She gave Edward the biggest crunchy-punch on his arm. The first one since she'd come to England.

'No! It's not flowers!' She wanted to tell him that it was the scent of a feeling. It was the explosion of happiness that Lady Jane felt when Puck came back. The same feeling she would feel when she went home to Maude [her old, old dog in Australia].

It was a reward for being away from something you loved for a very long time. Something that would make all the hard bits worthwhile.

But it was too difficult to tell about that now.

'Of course it's not flowers,' she giggled. 'There aren't any vases, you daft thing!'

Edward grinned. 'Hey! Did you hear that?' He looked at his mother. 'She sounds just like we do! Go on . . .' he said, pointing at Anne-Marie. 'Say "daft thing" again!'

He was teasing her but this time she didn't mind.

She was too full of the scent of flowers – and another feeling. A new feeling that was mixed up with a little ghost dog and a chapel in a church in a strange country.

And a boy who cared about her, even if she was different.

NETTE HILTON was born in Traralgon, Victoria, and has since lived in many different places in Australia and England. For many years she has combined her twin careers of teaching and writing. Her books include *A Proper Little Lady*, *The Web* and *The Long Red Scarf*, *The Belonging of Emmaline Harris* and *Four Eyes*. She lives surrounded by family and furred and feathered friends.

SHE JUST WANTS TO PLAY

SOPHIE MASSON

As soon as I came into the house, I knew someone was already there. Someone who shouldn't be there. Someone I couldn't see. Someone I couldn't smell, and that was worst of all.

It wasn't like that at our old house. Why did my Revered Ones have to move? I knew every corner of that old place, and I can tell you, no one who shouldn't be there was there! It was all clean fresh sunlight there, nothing hiding in dark corners, no shadows flitting so fast you couldn't catch them, no strange shivery pricklings of the air.

'Mum,' I hear my Sarah-girl say, 'what's the matter with Nan? Why is she growling like that, why are her legs so stiff?' I can't take any notice; I'm all eyes and ears and nose, trying to fix that thing in my mind, that thing that shouldn't be there.

I can feel it in the hall. I can feel it in the living-room. But most of all, I can feel it here, upstairs in this room, this bedroom where my Sarah-girl is to sleep. I won't let her.

Not till I've sorted out what to do about this stranger thing. It's so strong here, I can almost see it. The air is prickling around a particular spot. If I concentrate hard enough, I will see it. But I can't. And then I hear it move.

'Nan, what's the matter? Nan!' That's the sharp voice of my First Revered One, Sarah-girl's father. 'Stop it at once, or I'll tie you up outside!'

I try to calm down. It wouldn't do for them to tie me up where I can't protect them from the stranger who shouldn't be there. But I've got my eye on that ghostly spot. I'm not going to let it get away. It shifts. I can just see the movement. All the hair rises along my back. I can't help it.

'What is the matter with that dog? OK, Nan, that's enough. You're coming with me.'

I whimper, I yelp, but it's no good. He has me strongly by the collar, dragging me away from the room, and Sarah-girl will be left alone in there, with that thing! I can't allow it, no I can't! I wrench myself desperately from the hold of my Revered One, feeling very bad about it as I do so. I tear back along the hall and up the stairs to Sarah-girl's new room with him in hot pursuit. I've got to save her!

I come into the room, and Sarah-girl is standing looking out of the window. She turns when I come in and smiles. 'Are you OK, now, Nan? What was wrong?'

I lick her hand, but then I freeze. Something's odd. There's bright sunlight in the room, and Sarah-girl's shadow should be there, on that wall. And so it is. But next to hers – there's another. It's short and fat, with a long back and pointed ears, and a wide open mouth that is full of sharp teeth. I jump at the wall, I bark loudly, scraping my claws on the plaster. And of course Revered One comes in, then, sees me fall back from the wall, and the scratch marks on the plaster. But it's obvious he can't see the shadow.

'The dog's gone mad!' he shouts. 'Mad! Get away from her, Sarah!'

Sarah-girl turns her head to look at him. There is a strange green glint in there I've never seen before. 'It's OK, Dad,' she says, softly. 'She just wants to play.' She walks over to me, ruffles my coat, smiles innocently at her father. 'Isn't that right, Nan? It's OK, don't worry, I'll make sure she behaves. You're busy, Dad, with the unpacking.'

Puzzled, he looks into the new green glint of her eyes. He shakes his head, as if he'd dazed, and he says, meekly, 'Yes, I suppose I am. Well, I'd better get on with it.'

When he's gone, Sarah-girl turns to me. She whispers, 'She just wants to play, Nan. Don't be such an old bore. She knows all sorts of new games.'

New games! Ha! I don't trust that sort of play, I bark at the shadow cavorting on the wall. I don't like it at all! Get away from us!

'And if you won't play,' says Sarah-girl, startling me, her hands clenched in my fur, 'Well then, it'll just be the two of us, and you, Nan, locked up in the kennel out the back!'

I yelp. In the old house, Sarah-girl would never have talked to me like that. This house had already changed her. This tricksy house, with its tricksy, witchy ghost. I growl, Just wait, just wait, I'll watch you, and one day I'll get you!

Oh, I'm scared, I'm scared, comes the stranger's languid voice in my head. As if an old barking dog can get rid of me! Besides, I just want to play, that's all. I've not found a good playmate for three hundred years. And I like your Sarah-girl. She'll be my Sarah-girl, too, Nan-dog.

That makes me angry. I bark and bark, shouting that never, never will that happen, never will any ugly, stupid, nasty ghost cat ever compete for my Sarah-girl's affections! But the shadow on the wall just raises a lazy paw and swats my words away. Then it gathers itself in a spring and lands delicately on Sarah-girl's shoulder.

You'll have to get used to me, the stranger purrs. This is my house. It pauses. I could teach you some good games, it offers. Come on, old Nan-dog. We might as well get on.

Ha! A live cat is bad enough; a ghost cat perched on your Sarah-girl's shoulder; why, that is beyond the bounds of any decent thing! I turn my back on the ghost-cat, who is grinning at me like that picture in Sarah-girl's book. The indignity of it, a grin from someone who shouldn't even be there!

SOPHIE MASSON was born in Indonesia of French parents and brought up mainly in Australia. She is the prolific author of 30 novels in Australia for adults, young adults and children. Sophie has also had novels published in the United States, England and Germany, and numerous short stories around the world. Sophie lives in Armidale, New South Wales, with her husband and children. Her latest books include *In Hollow Lands* (Hodder Silver UK) and *Snow, Fire, Sword* (Random House Australia). Visit Sophie's website at www.northnet.comau/-smasson

DRAGON'S TOOTH

VICTOR KELLEHER

It was sticking out from the muddy bank of the creek: long and white, with a jagged, saw-like edge.

'What do you think it is?' Tim asked, rubbing mud and small crystals of frost from its sides.

His sister, Kate, after peering inquisitively over his shoulder, dismissed the thing with a wave of the hand.

'It's nothing but an old bone,' she said scornfully.

Tim wasn't so sure. It felt too sharp, too hard and shiny-white for a bone.

'It could be a . . . a sort of tooth,' he suggested.

'Whoever saw a tooth that sharp?' Kate answered. 'Why, even Spot thinks it's a bone.'

There was no denying that their dog, Spot, was interested in the newly found object. He was whining and jumping up excitedly, trying to snatch it from Tim's hand, a hungry gleam in his eyes.

'Well, I still think it's a tooth,' Tim said stubbornly. 'Probably from a . . . a dinosaur or something.'

And before Kate could contradict him, he shoved it safely into the side pocket of his anorak.

Within minutes, he and Kate had returned to their game of racing twig boats down the creek. Yet no matter how absorbed Tim became in their game, he never quite forgot about the tooth-like object nestling in his pocket. From time to time he reached in to touch it, as if to make certain it was still there – aware, as he did so, of Spot's eyes watching him hungrily.

Tim's desire to touch and hold the thing only increased as the day advanced.

'What's the matter with you?' Kate asked, sensing that something was wrong.

The same question was echoed by his mother later that evening.

'Oh, nothing much,' he said vaguely. 'Bit of a headache, that's all.'

'What you need is an early night,' his dad suggested slyly, fully expecting Tim to object.

But for once Tim agreed, and not only because he wanted to be alone with his discovery. In fact, he did feel rather odd, somehow different from normal.

'Yeah, I could do with a good night's sleep,' he said, pretending to yawn.

He didn't go straight off to bed, however. He paused briefly in the hallway, just long enough to snatch the tooth from his anorak. Spot was the only one who saw him do it, the dog growling deep in his throat and drawing back into the shadows.

Usually, at night, Tim read for a while; but on this particular night the lamplight worried his eyes. So he turned the lamp off and lay in the dark, the tooth cupped in both hands. It had a soothing effect on him. It made him feel bigger and stronger, and also less alone, as if he were really two people: himself, and someone or something else entirely.

It was the other self that he dreamed about. A gigantic creature who lay sprawled on a bed of gold, high in the mountains. All around him rose the ramparts of a castle, while sulphurous clouds pressed down from above. He knew that far below, in a distant valley, a boy called Tim slept restlessly; but throughout the long night he hardly spared the boy a thought.

The dream was finally brought to an end by a familiar voice.

'Come on, Tim! You're going to be late for school.'

'Yeah . . . coming, Mum,' he answered.

He climbed groggily out of bed and stood up, shielding his face from the morning sun which stung his eyes. He didn't feel unwell so much as different: his tongue thick and slimy, his skin strangely hot and dry.

'Step on it, Tim!' Kate called, adding her voice to Mum's.

Hurriedly, he slipped into his clothes, stowed the tooth in his school bag, and went downstairs. Breakfast was already on the table.

'Don't forget your lunch money,' his mother said, pointing to a small heap of coins beside his plate, and returned to the kitchen

The sight of the gleaming coins reminded him of his dream . . . and all at once the room seemed to vanish. He was back on the mountain top, breathing in the sulphurous air, the comforting touch of precious metal beneath him. He gave a deep rumbling sigh that shook the surrounding peaks.

From somewhere far off, he heard a scream.

'Mum! Mum! You'd better come in here!'

'What's going on?' a second voice answered.

He felt hands pushing roughly at him. He could hear hasty footsteps drawing nearer. He blinked . . . and blinked again . . . and straight away the dining room reappeared. To his surprise, he was perched up on the table, huddled over his lunch money as if it were a secret hoard.

'What on earth do you think you're doing?' his mother demanded.

'He's mad! That's what he is!' Kate cried.

'It's just . . . just a game,' he stammered. 'Messing about, that's all.'

He jumped down, his eyes fixed on Spot who continued to watch him from a distance, growling softly.

'Your father and I thought maybe you were sickening for something last night,' his mother said in a worried voice.

'No, I'm all right,' he insisted. 'Really.'

Grabbing his school bag and anorak, he rushed outside.

The morning was heavily overcast, the clouds low and threatening. Even so, he found the day far too bright and unpleasant. With his school bag slung across his shoulder, he dashed along the wintry streets, running faster than he ever had before. An unnatural strength seemed to flow through him, urging him to escape from this daylit world.

He felt better when he reached school, more secure within its dim interior. Throughout morning assembly, he hid in the toilets, crouched in the darkest corner. He didn't emerge until the start of the first period, when he slipped easily in amongst the other kids as they filed into class.

Soon after that the trouble began.

The lesson was maths, and he was given the task of handing out worksheets. All went well to begin with. Tim walked slowly between the desks, eyes downcast, handing out the sheets and saying nothing. Then someone switched on the overhead lights, and he clenched his eyes shut to protect them from the sudden glare. When he opened them, he was no longer standing in the classroom. The bright light, shining on the varnished desktops, had transformed them to shimmering gold. And he was back on the mountain top, his gold hoard spread out before him.

Mine, he thought fondly. All mine.

So that when a boyish hand reached out to touch the gold, he struck at it and bellowed with rage, thin streams of flame shooting from his nostrils.

There was a crash of falling chairs, followed by the sound of voices raised in alarm. With a rush, the brightly lit room returned, and he was gazing into the angry face of the teacher.

'What do you think you're . . .?' the teacher began, and stopped. 'Your eyes!' he went on, puzzled. 'What have you done to them? And that thing in your mouth, what is it?'

Beyond the teacher, Tim could see the terrified face of a boy, his eyebrows and hair lightly singed. The boy was staring down at the desk, its wooden surface scarred by deep claw marks.

Tim took a deep breath and blurted out the first excuse that came into his head.

'Er . . . it's . . . it's just a joke, sir. Some stuff I . . . I bought in one of those . . . er . . . you know, those game shops.'

'Well, this isn't my idea of a game!' the teacher said angrily. 'Go and get that stuff out of your eyes and mouth. Then report to the principal.'

'Yes, sir.'

He stumbled out to the toilets and stared into the mirror. Yet he already knew what to expect, so the deep green of his pupils caused him no real surprise. Nor did the forked black tongue that snaked from between his lips.

Clearly, he couldn't go to the principal. What he needed was somewhere dark and safe in which to hide. A stronghold he could defend against outsiders. What's more, he knew of just the place. Shoving the tooth inside his shirt, where it nestled cool against his fevered skin, he left the school at a run.

He felt even stronger now than he had before. Soon, he was leaping along rather than running; and at every bound thin tendrils of smoke drifted from his nostrils, billowing into the cold air like clouds of winter vapour.

It took him only minutes to reach home. As he ran upstairs, his mother called out:

'Is that you, Tim?'

By the time she reached the upstairs landing, he was crouched in his darkened room, the door locked, the curtains drawn.

'Go away!' he rumbled.

'Aren't you well?' she asked nervously. 'Should I call the doctor?'

'I need no one,' he croaked, his voice deeper still, small spurts of sulphurous flame shooting out into the room.

He heard her go downstairs and phone his father. But he no longer cared. The dimly lit room had almost ceased to exist. The darkened walls had taken on the appearance of rocky peaks; the ceiling had become a brooding sky; the yellowish bedside carpet shone like a pool of gold.

With a low rumble, he pulled up a trouser leg and inspected the coarse red scales forming on his skin. From inside his shoes there came a rasping sound, of claws scrabbling to be free. On his back, the space between his shoulder-blades started to bulge, as tiny wings thrust outwards.

He was so engrossed by these changes that he didn't hear his father enter the house. There was some hurried whispering on the stairs, and then the bedroom door burst open.

'So this is what you're up to!' his father shouted. 'Smoking on the sly!' He turned towards the door and called loudly: 'No wonder he doesn't feel well. You should just see this room. Full of cigarette smoke!'

Waving a hand to clear a path through the smoke, he strode over to the window and pulled the curtains. Tim, pained by the dazzle of light, leapt to his feet. Already his father was fumbling at the window catch.

'Leave it!' Tim roared, flames searing a path across the ceiling.

He dragged the tooth out from inside his shirt and brandished it like a weapon.

'Begone!' he bellowed in an unearthly voice.

But before he could launch himself at the helpless figure now flattened against the window, there was a flash of movement. It was Spot. Leaping through the open doorway, he clamped his jaws about the tooth and tore it from Tim's grasp.

'No!' Tim shrieked – so loud that the whole house trembled.

He made a desperate lunge for the dog, but it dodged and scampered downstairs, the tooth still in its mouth. When Tim tried to follow, the mountain top instantly faded; the precious pool of gold grew dim and vanished. And he was left in true darkness, everything blotted out as he slumped to the floor.

It was morning when he woke. The doctor was standing beside the bed, beaming down at him, his parents and sister looking on.

'There you are,' the doctor pronounced in a satisfied voice. 'Good as new. Just as I promised.'

'But those eyes...' his mother murmured uncertainly. 'They're still a bit... a bit... you know.'

'Oh, don't worry about that,' the doctor answered, heading for the door. 'It's the result of being over-tired, nothing else. Let him sleep, and it'll soon pass.'

Tim struggled up into a sitting position. He had only the vaguest memory of what had happened on the previous day. But just to be sure, he unbuttoned his pyjamas and peered down at his bare chest. There wasn't a sign of a scale anywhere.

'I'm feeling fine... I think,' he said in a puzzled voice.

'Is there anything we can get you?' Kate asked.

He was suddenly aware of a hollow feeling deep inside him – the kind of feeling that made him think of chips and roast dinners.

'Yeah... yeah. To tell you the truth, I'm starving.'

'That sounds more like the old Tim,' his father said, and they all laughed with relief, glad that everything was getting back to normal.

None of them bothered to look out of the window, to where Spot lay crouched on the back lawn. He was still mouthing the tooth – his eyes now a deep green; tufts of scaly looking feathers sprouting from his shoulders; plumes of smoke coiling from his nostrils like wintry vapour in the cool air.

VICTOR KELLEHER was born in London on 19 July 1939 and came to Australia in 1976 after living in South Africa and New Zealand. Victor's books have won and been shortlisted for many awards, including the Children's Book Council of Australia Book of the Year Award. His books include *Master of the Grove* (1982), *Taronga* (1986), *Beyond the Dusk* (2000) and *Goblin in the Bush* (2002). He now writes both children's and adult's novels full-time from his home in Bellingen, New South Wales.

30 AUSTRALIAN GHOST STORIES FOR CHILDREN

PAST LIVES

VASHTI FARRER

Of course, that's where cats are different from humans. We really do have nine lives. Nine chances, you might say, to get things right.

Every time we depart from one life, we somehow end up in another. And the funny thing is, I've managed to end up with the same mistress each time. Not that she's recognised me, of course, but I would have known her anywhere.

The first time was back in Ancient Egypt, in one of the fancy temples. She was young and slim then and she wore long slinky dresses and lots of eye make-up. I suspect she was really trying to look like us.

Anyway, she'd arrive each morning, clean out the golden bowls and fill them with sacred offal, that's liver and kidney, for your information. Then she'd top up our drink bowls with water from the Nile, or maybe asses' milk, as a treat. After that, she'd shake the sistrum rattles to call us and we'd come running from our sacred pillows.

And while we ate, she played beautiful music for us. Nothing too loud, mind, just soothing for the digestion. (Nowadays I have to listen to the TAB results and that's more likely to give me heartburn.)

But back then, it was an idyllic life, a pity it couldn't go on, but in the end some plague or other carried us off and we were buried underneath the temple. She was buried with us. Maybe the priests in the temple thought it was her fault we'd died or maybe they just wanted her to go on feeding us in the afterlife, who knows?

Anyway, we next met up in Europe, in the Middle Ages. We were living in this simple little cottage, trying to make ends meet. We shared the same food, whatever was going, a bit of bread and cheese, maybe, sometimes some soup. (Nowadays my dinner comes out of the big white cupboard with the light inside.)

Of course, back then I supplemented my diet with rats and mice I caught, but the funny thing was, although I often left one on the doorstep for her, she never seemed keen.

She was a kind-hearted woman and looked after everyone in the village. Cats and dogs would turn up with sore paws or runny eyes and she'd apply a bandage or bit of salve. Some even stayed on with us, cats I recognised from the old temple days and she gave them all names. There was Broke Leg, Bog Black, Dribble and Stump. Me she called Comely, because she said I was a handsome fellow.

Only it didn't last. The apothecary, a nasty piece of work, said she was ruining his business with her ointments and herbs and he called her a witch to her face. Well, from then on, every time a horse got sick or a cow had trouble giving birth, they said it was her fault, that she'd put the evil eye on it.

Soon, the whole village had turned against her and they tied her to a ducking stool and dunked her in the village pond, down and up, down and up, till she was gasping for breath and nearly drowned. And then they burnt her.

Of course, they soon realised their mistake. And afterwards, people would look wistfully at the cottage where she'd lived and cats and dogs would turn sadly away when a stranger opened the door.

Broke Leg, Bog Black, Dribble and Stump had to find new homes. I befriended the Burgomaster's cook and managed to rid her kitchen of mice and rats. So she gave me scraps and let me sleep near the stove, but it wasn't the same.

And now I'm in this life and I'm with her again. You'd think she would have learnt by now, but humans never do. She's still feeding all the neighbours' animals whenever they go away and taking in all sorts of thin and neglected creatures to give them a home. There's hardly room to move at times.

There's been a change with the rats and mice, too. She hates to see them killed and dumped on the doorstep like before. 'Naughty boy, let it go,' she shouted only yesterday when I had a particularly nasty customer by the scruff of the neck. And I knew him from a past life too. He was the beady-eyed foreman in the cook's kitchen till he met his death at my paws.

Yet there she was, wringing her hands, and telling me to stop. I wanted to say, 'Leave off woman! This is cat's business,' but my mouth was full and I knew if I spoke I'd lose the blighter.

Of course, I could have put in for a fancy household this time round, with an electric blanket of my own. But I'm a softie too. I get to sleep on her bed, alongside

Broke Leg, Bog Black, Dribble and Stump (yes, they're all back too). Only they have different names this time and don't look quite the same, which is probably just as well, since they're all black this time round and that might have caused a real problem back in the Middle Ages.

But the t.l.c.'s still there. Sometimes it's even embarrassing. Like the time I had a sore eye and she called out, 'Oh bubba-lulu, time for some cream in your eyebe-jybie!' I mean, honestly, baby-talk! Whatever happened to dignity? I could hear the rats sniggering under the floor boards. Mind you, they don't snigger when she says, 'Elevenses!' Then I'm sure their greedy little eyes are glowing red in the dark.

And while she looks after us, we all keep an eye on her. There's none of us getting any younger and I don't have many years to go, but I tell you, I wouldn't mind putting in for a fourth time with her. Only by then we'll probably all be in high-rise apartments with high-rise cat boxes and not enough room to swing a rat, not to mention pretend meat and plastic kitty litter.

I'm used to listening to the TAB results now. It's taken me a while and it's not music to my ears, but she likes to listen and sometimes next day there's a treat on the menu for us, so it must be music to her.

I've seen better days, and worse, for that matter. Now things are just different. But the way I see it, there's comfort in a bit of mess. A bed's not really right when it's totally flat, it needs a bit of mussing up, even if you do have to share.

After all, life's one big bed and we've all got to circle round a bit to make it ours.

VASHTI FARRER writes short stories for adults and plays, poetry and stories for primary and secondary school students. She is a regular contributor to *School Magazine*. Vashti is best known for her historical novels for young readers, which include *Escape to Eaglehawk*, *Eureka Gold* and *Ned's Kang-u-roo*. One of her books in the *My Story* series, *Plagues and Federation — the Diary of Kitty Barnes*, is set in the Rocks area of Sydney in 1900. Vashti loves theatre, acting, history, archaeology and unusual characters.

FLUFF ON THE BRAIN

ANITA BELL

'Dad, come quick!' I screamed, racing for the commotion in the back yard. I couldn't wait for his help. I could smell blood and I waded into the fight by myself, scrunching through knee deep crusty mulberry leaves to get to my dogs. Our two shepherds were waging war over a lump of white fluff which could only be one thing. I grabbed Girlie's collar first. She had dropped the little rabbit for an instant to get a better hold on its neck and she hadn't expected me to wrench her away. I dragged her, snapping and snarling to the other side of the yard and scrambled for the chain to her dog house.

She wouldn't sit still and it took me a few attempts to click onto the collar while I shouted at her and called for more help. *Where was everyone when you needed them?* I ran back for Major, my heart sinking with every step.

Ten metres never felt so far!

By the time I reached him, it was too late. He looked up with his big brown happy eyes and drooled his triumph at me.

'Bad dog!' I cried. 'You're a bad, naughty dog!'

Major whimpered, then drooled happily at me as if I was some kind of strange confusing human that didn't recognise a doggy hero when I saw one.

I ignored him and looked at the little corpse at my feet. Fluff was the neighbour's pet. Robbie Milkiner was an only child and the little rabbit was his only friend – or at least it had been. My dogs had *murdered* it!

I looked along the battered chain wire fence that divided our backyard from theirs, and my frown dragged my ears down. The little rabbit had escaped its pen many times before. Usually, it would sit at the bottom of their back steps, waiting for Robbie to find him, nibbling on daisies and swatting at butterflies. But this time, the little pet must have found the big rusted hole in the wire behind my mum's rose garden.

Major picked up the body and shook it, dropping it again at my feet. 'Wasn't I pleased?' he seemed to say. Didn't I understand that he'd saved us all from a savage, marauding rabbit? I scowled my nastiest scowl at him and tied him up beside Girlie.

I had to do something.

Mum had taken my brother to the football finals and Dad was obviously still enjoying his favourite Saturday past time – sleeping in front of the TV.

That left everything up to me.

I scratched my head as if the answer was living there with my cooties and I chased them round my hair a few times with my fingers. What could I do? The pocket money I'd been saving for my new roller skates was enough for a new rabbit. I could buy one and hope that nobody noticed the difference, but the pet shop was waaayyyy over on the other side of town. There was no chance at all that I could buy a fake Fluff with my pocket money before Robbie's parents came home from their morning shopping. But if anyone suspected that my dogs had been the murderers, then the dog catcher would take them away and make sure they were put to sleep – forever! Everybody knows that's what happens to killer dogs!

I certainly couldn't let *that* happen.

Girlie and Major were two of the sweetest dogs you could ever imagine. Everybody said so! And besides, the deed was done. There was no point in letting two more good animals die. I'd feel haunted forever!

I had to protect them.

I picked up the battered little corpse and I headed quickly for my house.

Dad was in the lounge room, snoring like our old lawnmower. I crept past him and went straight to the bathroom where I washed, shampooed and blow-dried the little rabbit's body, taking great care to brush out all the tangles in his long white fur. I even painted his little claws shiny black with one of my big sister's punk coloured fingernail polish. Then I sneaked past Dad again with the little rabbit and ran outside. One big hop from me and I was over the fence where I could put Fluff safely back in his cage. Then I heard the car.

It was Robbie's parents.

I bolted for their garden shed, hiding behind a giant thorny thicket of blackberries, dodging savage little thorns and praying that nobody could see me. Plastic bag after plastic bag of groceries were taken inside until finally the Milkiners' car was empty. They all went inside. The door closed. And the yard fell silent.

I dashed for the fence. I leapt . . . and I made it!

All afternoon I hung around outside, waiting for Fluff's mysterious death to be discovered. But it wasn't to be. Robbie didn't go out to play that day – or the day after that. I had to wait a whole week with Fluff on my brain, worrying if my dogs were going to be blamed for the murder. I imagined ghosts of Fluff coming back to haunt me every night. I saw ghosts of Fluff out of the corner of my eye on my way to school every day and on the way home again every afternoon. I saw Fluff in the bathroom where I brushed and cleaned him. I saw Fluff in the backyard teasing and poking faces at my dogs and I saw Fluff, waiting at the bottom of the steps next door swatting butterflies and waiting for Robbie . . . until one afternoon, I overheard my Dad having a beer over the back fence with Robbie's Dad.

'It's the strangest thing,' Mr Milkiner said. 'Fluff died of old age. We buried him in our garden here beside the fence, and then three days later, there he was – back in his cage, and except for being *dead*, he looked better than ever!'

I only saw Fluff's ghost once after that. He poked his little rabbit nose up at me, as if teasing and pleased that he had the last laugh.

VOICES FROM BEYOND

A short story based on the story arc for *Crystal Coffin* and *Kirby's Crusaders*

ANITA BELL

Kirby slid under a dark thicket of lantana, thorns clawing her flesh as she listened to the crunch of leaves in the forest around her. Moon shadows danced like wicked spirits on the breeze, stars winking out as storm clouds boiled on the far side of the lake and mountains.

A horse whinnied deeper in the forest and Kirby stiffened, hoping her black mare would finish laying a false trail without getting caught riderless on her way home. But a twig snapped in the scrub to Kirby's left, leaves rustled to her right and she glanced from side to side, too cautious to turn her head in case the movement gave her position away to her stalkers.

Two of them, she noticed, both managing to track her around the boathouse and clearing before heading inland. One circled in from the east, the other from the west and Kirby frowned, wondering how she'd ever manage to slip away from them.

'I have a plan,' snickered a ghostly whisper close to her ear. A silvery hand touched Kirby's shoulder but she shrugged it off like acid rain.

'Quiet!' Kirby scolded and the dwarf-like spirit dissolved from one side of her to reappear again on the other. 'Your plans are insane,' Kirby snarled. 'Bug off back to the underworld, before you give me away!'

'Trust me,' insisted the whisperer. 'Ten years since your birth. Have I ever failed?'

Don't get me started, Kirby wanted to say, but she held her tongue silent. For as long as she could remember, the spirit's smug round face had always cooed to her, reassuring at first, like the doting mother that she'd lost soon after her birth. But the spirit had also been changing. Kirby realised it now in the heartbeat it took to notice that the wide silver eyes used to be blue. The dwarf-spirit seemed shorter too, with squat body shrinking ever closer to the ground – almost as fast as Kirby's slim skeletal frame had grown taller – each tick of the clock stretching their differences, as if melting energy away from one to create the other.

The spirit's lips curled into a grin and Kirby shivered.

Footsteps padded closer, rustling lightly in the crumpled leaf litter.

Kirby held her breath, glaring warnings at the spirit to stay silent until they passed – denim jeans, knees bent – the two boys hunting her like two dingoes after a hare. No torch lights, except for the occasional red blink far out on the water where her father fished in a small boat with their neighbour. No voices either except for the odd grumble when one caught a trout bigger than the other.

Kirby's hunters signalled each other, tapping fingers to their noses before heading off to follow the sound of her horse into the forest.

'This way,' the spirit urged, tugging Kirby back towards the boathouse. 'Hide where they least expect you.'

Kirby scowled at the risk, her feet digging in, but the spirit slapped the leaves making noise like a hurried breeze. No safety under the bush any more if her hunters heard it. Kirby bolted for the shed, her head down, long black hair whipping her back as she headed for the door. Waves lapped the sandy shore like cheerleaders as she went in. Darkness clamped her inside like a warm damp glove. The stench of dried fish guts assaulted her and the dwarf-spirit clenched both their noses shut with ghostly fingers.

'There,' ordered the spirit, pointing at the floor – too dark to see in the middle of the room without light, but they both remembered the trap door.

'But my brother got stuck down there!' Kirby complained. 'He was lost all night and day when he tried to hide there!'

'That was months ago,' snorted the dwarf-spirit. 'He got stuck because of his height. But you're smaller. You'll fit easy!'

Kirby baulked – until ghostly fingers grabbed her clothes and hauled her towards the trap door. Kirby's head stung with panic.

'Even if you do get stuck,' cooed the spirit as it lifted the lid, 'your dad will be back by midnight and he'll find you. He stashes his flare-gun down there, remember?'

The spirit shoved forward and Kirby stumbled as she fell in.

'Ouch!' she cried as her knee grazed, arm twisted and her forehead cracked in the pit of darkness. Time passed, eons and seconds folding back on each other. Voices called to her from beyond the black void of unconsciousness. Her mother's song, her father's cry, her brother's yell, her cousin's shout, all blending one into the other within the dream, like carollers singing in distant-tune with the dwarf-spirit. Kirby tried to move but couldn't, tried to open her mouth to shout but in her mind and dream she screamed only silence.

'Your fault!' she cried without making a sound in the real world. 'You get me in trouble all the time now!'

'No!' argued the spirit appearing again above her. 'I would have stopped if I'd foreseen it.'

'You shoved me!' Kirby swore, but she received no answer.

The dwarf-spirit tried to peer at the bump near Kirby's ear, but Kirby shrugged the hand away, causing static to zap from her ear to the spirit. Silver eyes turned blue, then silver, then zigzagged all over as the source of the voice blurred like interference on a TV channel.

'You're a ghost,' Kirby insisted. 'You can see everything!'

'I can't!' cried the dwarf-spirit. 'I never said I was a ghost. What gave you that idea?'

'You're dead,' Kirby argued. 'You've always whispered it's so. How can you be dead – and here – and be something other than a ghost? What else is there?'

The spirit slumped on her knees. 'A memory,' she confessed, 'a digital image of someone dead who shouldn't be.'

'Liar!' Kirby cried. 'There's no such technology!'

'There is,' insisted the spirit. 'I'm the un-living proof. Now, be still!' she cursed as Kirby jerked to escape her coma.

Images of her mother flooded Kirby's memory. Static hissed sparks in the dark again and the spirit touched a tiny hair inside Kirby's lobe as if adjusting a wire connection. 'At least this bump on your head explains why transmission's been warping over the years – malfunctioning I think, from the implant connections stretching as you grow.'

'But who . . . ?' Kirby sighed as her body drifted back to reality. 'Why me?'

'Because you fell into the hole, silly,' laughed her brother and her cousin squatted to giggle down at her too.

'Get up,' snarled her father. He brushed long black hair over Kirby's ear as if hiding it as he bundled her over his shoulder. 'Say your prayers,' he whispered. 'You'll need more help soon, my girl, than anyone living can give you.'

ANITA BELL was ten when she first recognised that her parents were being ripped off. She made her first long-term business decision when she was twelve, managed her parents' farm when they were away on business soon after that, signed a contract to buy her own land when she was sixteen – and she owned it debt free within a year, before she even earned her first provisional licence! Anita learned to survive the hard way. But she also learned early on that age is no barrier to success and the power to control it is already inside you. You just have to shake it away now and then and figure out when to listen to that little voice inside that's supposed to keep you safe. Her *Kirby's Crusaders* series helps you figure it out, mixing fun, finance and fiction for the first time ever!

BIRDSCRAP

From *Unbelievable!*
PAUL JENNINGS

1

The twins sat on the beach throwing bits of their lunch to the seagulls.

'I don't like telling a lie to Grandma,' said Tracy. 'It wouldn't be fair. She has looked after us since Mum and Dad died. We would be in a children's home if it wasn't for her.'

Gemma sighed, 'We won't be hurting Grandma. We will be doing her a favour. If we find Dad's rubies we can sell them for a lot of money. Then we can fix up Seagull Shack and give Grandma a bit of cash as well.'

'Why don't you wait until we are eighteen? Dad's will says that we will own Seagull Shack then. We can even go and live there if you want to,' replied Tracy.

Gemma started to get cross. 'I've told you a million times. We won't be eighteen for another three years. The last person who hiked in to Seagull Shack said that it was falling to pieces. If we wait that long the place will be blown off the cliff or wrecked by vandals. Then we'll never find the rubies. They are inside that shack. I'm sure Dad hid them inside before he died.'

Tracy threw another crust to the seagulls. 'Well, what are you going to tell Grandma, then?'

'We tell her that we are staying at Surfside One camping ground for the night. Then we set out for Seagull Shack by hiking along the cliffs. If we leave in the morning we can get there in the afternoon. We spend the night searching the house for the rubies. If we find them, Grandma will have a bit of money in the bank and we can send in some builders by boat to fix up Seagull Shack.'

'Listen,' said Tracy to her sister. 'What makes you think we are going to find the rubies? The place was searched after Dad died and neither of them was found.'

'Yes, but it wasn't searched by us. We know every corner of that shack. And we knew Dad. We know how his mind worked. We can search in places no one else would think of. I think I know where they are anyway. I have an idea. I think Dad hid them in the stuffed seagull. I had a dream about it.'

'Hey, did you see that?' yelled Tracy without warning. 'Where did that crust go?'

'What crust?'

'I threw a crust to the seagulls and it vanished.'

'Rubbish,' said Gemma, 'One of the birds got it. Bread doesn't just vanish.'

Tracy threw another scrap of bread into the air. It started to fall to the ground and then stopped as if caught by an invisible hand. It rose high above their heads, turned and headed off into the distance. All the other gulls flapped after it, squawking and quarrelling as they went.

'Wow,' shrieked Gemma. 'How did you do that?'

'I didn't,' said Tracy slowly. 'Something flew off with it. Something we can't see. Something invisible. Perhaps a bird.'

Gemma started to laugh. 'A ghost gull maybe?'

'That's not as funny as you think,' said Tracy. 'It's a sign. Some thing or some one wants us to go to Seagull Shack.'

'Maybe you've got it wrong,' replied Gemma. 'Maybe something doesn't want us to go to Seagull Shack.'

The wind suddenly changed to the south west and both girls shivered.

2

Two days later Tracy and Gemma struggled along the deserted and desolate clifftops. They were weighed down with hiking packs and water bottles. Far below them the Southern Ocean swelled and sucked at the rocky cliff. Overhead the blue sky was broken only by a tiny white seagull which circled slowly in the salt air.

'How far to go?' moaned Gemma. 'My feet are killing me. We've been walking for hours.'

'It's not far now,' said Tracy. 'Just around the next headland. We should be able to see the brown roof any moment . . . Hey. What was that?' She felt her hair and pulled out some sticky white goo. Then she looked up at the seagull cirling above. 'You rotten fink,' she yelled at it. 'Look at this. That seagull has hit me with bird droppings.'

Gemma lay down on the grassy slope and started to laugh. 'Imagine that,' she gasped. 'There are miles and miles of clifftop with no one around and that bird has to drop its dung right on your head.' Her laughter stopped abruptly as something splotted into her eye. 'Aaaaagh, it's hit me in the eye. The stupid bird is bombing us.'

They looked up and saw that there were now four or five birds circling above. One of them swooped down and released its load. Another white splodge hit Tracy's head. The other birds followed one after the other, each dropping its foul load into one of the girls' hair. They put their hands on top of their heads and started to run. More and more birds gathered, circling, wheeling and diving above the fleeing figures. Bird droppings rained down like weighted snow.

The girls stumbled on. There was no shelter on the exposed wind-swept cliffs – there was no escape from the guano blizzard that engulfed them.

Tracy stumbled and fell. Tears cut a trail through the white mess on her face. 'Come on,' cried Gemma. Keep going – we must find cover.' She dragged her sister to her feet and both girls groped their way through the white storm being released from above by the squealing, swirling gulls.

Finally, exhausted and blinded, the twins collapsed into each other's arms. They huddled together and tried to protect themselves from the pelting muck by holding their packs over their heads. Gemma began to cough. The white excrement filled her ears, eyes and nostrils. She had to fight for every breath.

And then, as quickly as it had begun, the attack ended. The whole flock sped out to sea and disappeared over the horizon.

The girls sat there panting and sobbing. Each was covered in a dripping white layer of bird dung. Finally Gemma gasped. 'I can't believe this. Look at us. Covered in bird droppings. Did that really happen? Where have they gone?' She looked anxiously out to sea.

'They've probably run out of ammo,' said Tracy. 'We had better get to the shack as quick as we can before they come back.'

3

An hour later the two girls struggled up to the shack. It sat high above the sea, perched dangerously on the edge of a cliff which fell straight to the surging ocean beneath. Its battered tin roof and peeling wooden walls stood defiantly against the might of the ocean winds.

Both girls felt tears springing to their eyes. 'It reminds me of Dad and all those fishing holidays we had here with him,' said Tracy. They stood there on the old porch for a moment, looking and remembering.

'This won't do,' said Gemma as she unlocked the door and pushed it open. 'Let's get cleaned up and start looking for those two rubies.'

Inside was much as they remembered it. There were only two rooms: a kitchen with an old table and three chairs and fishing rods and nets littered around; and a bedroom with three mattresses on the floor. The kitchen also contained a sink and an old sideboard with a huge, stuffed seagull standing on it. It had only one leg and a black patch on each wing. It stared out of one of the mist-covered windows at the sky and the waves beyond.

'It almost looks alive,' shivered Tracy. 'Why did Dad shoot it anyway? He didn't believe in killing birds.'

'It was wounded,' answered Gemma. 'So he put it out of its misery. Then he stuffed it and mounted it because it was so big. He said it was the biggest gull he had ever seen.'

'Well,' said Tracy. 'I'm glad you're the one who is

going to look inside it for the rubies, because I'm not going to touch it. I don't like it.'

'First,' said Gemma, 'we clean off all this muck. Then we start searching for the rubies.' The two girls cleaned themselves with tank water from the tap in the sink. Then they sat down at the table and looked at the stuffed seagull. Gemma cut a small slit in its belly and carefully pulled out the stuffing. A silence fell over the hut and the clifftop. Not even the waves could be heard.

The air seemed to be filled with silent sobbing.

'The rubies aren't there,' said Gemma at last. She put the stuffing back in the dead bird and placed it on its stand. 'I'm glad that's over,' she went on. 'I didn't like the feel of it. It gave me bad vibes.'

As the lonely darkness settled on the shack, the girls continued their hunt for the rubies. They lit a candle and searched on into the night without success. At last, too tired to go on, Tracy unrolled her sleeping bag and prepared for bed. She walked over to the window to pull across the curtain but froze before reaching it. A piercing scream filled the shack. 'Look,' she shrieked. 'Look.'

Both girls stared in terror at the huge seagull sitting outside on the window sill. It gazed in at them, blinking every now and then with fiery red eyes. 'I can see into it,' whispered Gemma. 'I can see its gizzards. It's transparent.'

The lonely bird stared, pleaded with them silently and then crouched on its single leg and flapped off into the moonlight.

Before either girl could speak, a soft pitter-patter began on the tin roof. Soon it grew louder until the shack was filled with a tremendous drumming. 'What a storm,' yelled Gemma.

'It's not a storm,' Tracy shouted back. 'It's the birds. The seagulls have returned. They are bombing the house.'

She stared in horror at the ghostly flock that filled the darkness with ghastly white rain.

All through the night the drumming on the roof continued. Towards the dawn it grew softer but never for a moment did it stop. Finally the girls fell asleep, unable to keep their weary eyes open any longer.

4

At 10am Tracy awoke in the darkness and pressed on the light in her digital watch. 'Wake up,' she yelled. 'It's getting late.'

'It can't be,' replied Gemma. 'It's still dark.'

The shack was as silent as a tomb. Gemma lit a candle and went over to the window. 'Can't see a thing,' she said.

Tracy pulled open the front door and shrieked as a wave of bird droppings gushed into the room. It oozed into the kitchen in a foul stream. 'Quick,' she yelled. 'Help me shut the door or we'll be drowned in the stuff.'

Staggering, grunting and groaning, they managed to shut the door and stop the stinking flow. 'The whole house is buried,' said Gemma. 'And so are we. Buried alive in bird droppings.'

'And no one knows we are here,' added Tracy.

They sat and stared miserably at the flickering candle. All the windows were blacked out by the pile of dung that covered the house.

'There is no way out,' moaned Gemma.

'Unless . . .' murmured Tracy, 'they haven't covered the chimney.' She ran over to the fireplace and looked up. 'I can see the sky,' she exclaimed. 'We can get up the chimney.'

It took a lot of scrambling and shoving but at last the

two girls sat perched on the top of the stone chimney. They stared in disbelief at the house, which was covered in a mountain of white bird droppings. The chimney was the only evidence that underneath the oozing pile was a building.

'Look,' said Gemma with outstretched hand. 'The transparent gull.' It sat, alone on the bleak cliff, staring at the shaking twins. 'It wants something,' she said quietly.

'And I know what it is,' said Tracy. 'Wait here.' She eased herself back down the chimney and much later emerged carrying the stuffed seagull.

'Look closely at that ghost gull,' panted Tracy. 'It's only got one leg. And it has black patches on its wings. And look how big it is. It's this bird.' She held up the stuffed seagull. 'It's the ghost of this stuffed seagull. It wants its body back. It doesn't like being stuffed and left in a house. It wants it returned to nature.'

'Okay,' Gemma yelled at the staring gull. 'You can have it. We don't want it. But first we have to get down from here.' The two girls slid, swam, and skidded their way to the bottom of the sticky mess. Then, like smelly white spirits, the sisters walked to the edge of the cliff with the stuffed bird. The ghost seagull sat watching and waiting.

Tracy pulled the stuffed seagull from the stand and threw it over the cliff into the air that it had once loved and lived in. Its wings opened in the breeze and it circled slowly, like a glider, and after many turns crashed on a rock in the surging swell beneath.

The ghost gull lifted slowly into the air and followed it down until it came to rest on top of the still, stuffed corpse.

'Look,' whispered Tracy in horror. 'The ghost gull is pecking at the stuffed one. It's pecking its head.'

A wave washed across the rock and the stuffed seagull

vanished into the foam. The ghost gull flapped into the breeze and then flew above the girls' heads. 'It's bombing us,' shouted Gemma as she put her hands over her head.

Two small shapes plopped onto the ground beside them.

'It's the eyes of the stuffed seagull,' said Tracy in a hoarse voice.

'No it's not,' replied Gemma. 'It's Dad's rubies.'

They sat there, stunned, saying nothing and staring at the red gems that lay at their feet.

Tracy looked up. 'Thank you, ghost gull,' she shouted.

But the bird had gone and her words fell into the empty sea below.

PAUL JENNINGS was born near London, in 1943, and was six when he came to live in Melbourne with his parents and sister. After he left school he went to Frankston Teachers College and taught for a while before studying to become a speech pathologist. Then he worked as a Lecturer in Special Education before moving to the Warrnambool Institute of Adult Education in 1979 to work as a Senior Lecturer in Language and Literature. He stayed there for ten years until he began writing full-time. His books have won many awards and he was appointed a Member in the General Division of the Order of Australia (AM) in the Australia Day 1995 Honours List for service to children's literature.

THE HAUNTING OF CLAYTON QUINN

From *Party Animals*
CHRISTINE HARRIS

Clayton Quinn didn't actually see him at first. He sensed him. A shiver ran down Clayton's spine. Although he was alone in the bedroom, he couldn't shake the feeling that he was being watched.

He rolled off the bed and stood, eyes alert. Nothing: there was nothing different. Puzzled, he walked to the window and looked out. There was no one there and nowhere to hide. The garden consisted of smooth lawns and neat beds of brightly-coloured petunias. You couldn't hide yourself under those unless you were an elf. There was no one visible on the street outside. Clayton shrugged. Perhaps his imagination had deceived him.

The second time it happened, Clayton had woken feeling groggy. He hadn't slept well the night before; tossing and turning, feeling hot then cold. Then there was the eerie sound of plovers calling to each other in the darkness, and the bright gaze of a full moon that the curtains couldn't fully blot out.

This time it was more than a feeling. There was a movement: a shift of light, a change in the atmosphere, a shadow – something.

'Hello?' he called out in a first-thing-in-the-morning croaky voice. There was no reply. Had it been the vague echo of a dream?

The next incident occurred as Clayton stood in front of the bedroom mirror. He smoothed the thick brown hair back from his face, then shook his head.

'Nerd!' he said aloud and mussed it all up again with strong fingers. The reflection that looked back at him had locks of hair squirming in all directions. 'That's better.'

As Clayton stared at the familiar face in the glass he thought he saw something behind him. He spun round.

'Who's there?'

There was no answer. Slowly, eyes wide, Clayton turned back to the mirror and waited. Had it been the shadow of a bird whizzing past the window? They did that sometimes: dive-bombed the glass outside, either because they saw insects or fell in love their own reflection and thought it was another bird.

But even as he asked himself all the sensible questions about birds, clouds, anything that might cause a shift of light, he knew he was fooling himself. He hadn't seen any of those things. It had been the figure of a person reflected behind him. Shady, indistinct, but definitely a human shape. He had seen no features, no hands, nothing to suggest a personality or identity, just a shadow. And it wasn't his.

He stood still. There was no more movement reflected. Something about mirrors. He thought hard, then it came to him. Once he'd read a book called OUTER FACE which told a story about a mirror door. A ghost and a girl communicated through that door. It was a connection between their worlds. Perhaps the mirror in front of him was a key to contacting this strange presence.

Reaching out, he gently touched his fingertips to the cold, smooth surface of the glass. Despite feeling like a complete idiot, he ran his fingers all over the mirror then spoke to his image, which also had its hands up.

'Is anyone in there?'

He pressed his ear to the glass and listened. Nothing: just the ordinary fuzzy sounds of an ear. 'I'd like to talk to you,' he tried again. The only result was a fine mist blurring the lower part of his reflected face as his breath condensed on the cold surface. Clayton pushed away from the mirror and his image followed. He screwed up his nose. 'I give up.'

Although his efforts at communication had failed, he knew a presence was there, haunting his consciousness. Gradually Clayton became accustomed to the feeling that, at times, someone else was in the bedroom. He even expected it. And he stopped jumping at the shift of light in the mirror and the hazy outline of a figure.

It didn't speak to him or touch him. In fact, it was no bother. The thing was there and not there simultaneously. Until the morning Clayton turned from the window and saw the face of a boy staring at him.

The face floated on shadowy shoulders and arms, but below that, it seemed to disappear into nothing. Or perhaps the boy was just transparent. Through his body and legs Clayton saw the bed and bookshelves along the other wall.

Uncertain, the apparition peered at him. He had clear, pale skin, large dark eyes, and seemed about the same age as Clayton.

The boy looked the sort who would laugh easily if something funny happened. But right now he was deadly serious. Clayton could understand why. There was nothing remotely humorous about seeing straight through the body of a stranger. And there was something about the odd way he stared that made Clayton suspect he appeared equally strange to the other boy.

Clayton smiled. The transparent boy tilted his head and didn't respond at first. Then the corners of his mouth lifted.

Suddenly, he glanced behind him as though a sound had caught his attention. He turned back to Clayton and shrugged an apology, then faded. Disappeared would have been the wrong way to put it. He didn't go suddenly, just paled into invisibility like Clayton's breath on the mirror minutes earlier. Clayton was curious, and he sensed the boy felt the same about him. He wanted to see him again.

His wish was fulfilled much sooner than he'd anticipated. The visitor materialised again, and he wasn't alone. Beside his, with a face distorted by terror, was a woman. She made no sound, but her mouth opened and Clayton could see rows of silver fillings in her back teeth as she screeched.

This time there was no gentle fade. Clayton Quinn vanished, annoyed at being at the centre of such unwarranted fuss. He was only learning. He sometimes made mistakes. Given time, he'd get the hang of it. Couldn't they give a ghost a chance?

CHRISTINE HARRIS writes anywhere – at her desk or in Pizza Huts, in motels and on planes, on the beach and in bed. She loves eating chocolate and brie cheese, discovering new flowers in her cottage garden and telling stories. Christine has written more than 30 books including short stories, science fiction, historical novels, picture books and poetry. Her work has been published in Australia and internationally.

THE SCENT OF VIOLETS

ELIZABETH HUTCHINS

'Gordon, there's a child here – by the school crossing!' called my teacher, Miss Johns.

Gordon our driver screeched to a halt as a girl with a backpack drifted out from the twilight shadows by the old bridge, almost stepping in front of our bus. 'Little idiot!' he swore. 'Anyway – ' he turned to Miss Johns, 'I thought no one was coming from Pontville School.' But he let the girl in, and she quietly slipped into the seat next to me. A blast of cold air seemed to follow her, even though it was a warm evening.

While Gordon gave her a lecture about road sense, Miss Johns was checking the camp list. The girl said her name was Ellen Francis. 'I don't know – your name's not here,' Miss Johns shrugged in a puzzled manner, 'but I'll contact your school tomorrow.'

We had been picked up from half a dozen country schools, and were heading south for a writing camp at famous Anstey House. Except for Chad and Cameron from my school, Oatlands, who laughed and joked non-stop, we all seemed shy.

I glanced at Ellen's long black hair and pale skin, wishing I could look so cool. 'My name's Jade,' I said; but she just stared right through me. It was a relief when we finally pulled up in front of the grand old mansion that was to be our home for two days.

'Nobody's here,' someone giggled. 'This is creepy.' We were left standing in a nervous mob by the big front door, Gordon and Miss Johns having disappeared. It was dark now except for a full moon rising.

'Just knock,' said Ellen. 'They're waiting for us.'

How did she know that? When Chad thumped on the door, it swung open silently. Then a woman holding a candle and wearing a long crinoline and a shawl quavered, 'Welcome, young writers! Come in.'

Of course, this got us into the mood for an evening of spooky ghost stories and gory tales of betrayal and murder. We were given candles before being taken to our bedrooms, then told to report to the ballroom in 'suitable attire' in ten minutes. That meant the costumes from colonial days which we had been instructed to improvise.

Ellen and I were given a chilly, shadowy little room in the tower. As I struggled into the long skirt and satin jacket that I had borrowed from my grandmother, Ellen shivered. 'There is a very sad presence in this room,' she announced. 'Can't you feel it?'

I concentrated hard. 'Not really,' I said finally. 'But there's a sweet smell – like violets.'

On entering the elegant old ballroom we were ushered over to the huge fireplace. In the flickering light I could now see all my fellow campers, including a newly arrived group of Hobart kids. Everyone had made some effort to look old-fashioned, with a cloak, waistcoat or long skirt. But it was Ellen who made me gasp. She looked as if she really had stepped out of the past, in her flowing skirt of green silk, with a black velvet bodice over a white lacy blouse. Her violet bonnet too was edged with hand-made lace.

Miss Johns had noticed her too. 'Ellen! Who made your stunning costume?' she asked.

'Why, my mother did,' Ellen replied in a refined voice. She looked a bit surprised, as if to say, 'Don't mothers always make their children's clothes?'

I could see by her prim demeanour that she had already worked her way into the role of a girl from long ago.

Gordon, who was camp leader, reminded us that we had been chosen as the best writers from our schools. Tonight we would tell tales and relive days long past; and tomorrow we would write. He urged us to enter into the spirit of the house.

'Many years ago,' he began, 'Anstey House was owned by a rich merchant called Holland, who – '

He went on to tell us of Mary-Anne, the little maid who fell in love with Mr Holland's handsome son Richard. She used to watch for him from her bedroom up in the tower, then creep out and meet him in the summerhouse.

'The tower! That's our bedroom!' I whispered to Ellen, who nodded, wide-eyed.

'But one night,' Gordon continued, 'Richard brought home a beautiful lady, and Mary-Anne saw him kissing his new love down by the lake in the moonlight. In her grief she flung herself from the top of the tower . . .' A shudder went round the room.

'. . . and it is said that her ghost still appears at full moon.'

That set the tone for the evening. Of course, some stories worked, and some didn't. A few kids were too nervous to take part, while Cameron's yarn was strewn with mangled, headless bodies. I told my grandmother's tale about the little boy in a blue jacket who was seen sometimes standing at her dressing table, sorting a pile of buttons. Everyone clapped politely, but I knew it fell flat.

And then it was Ellen's turn.

'My name is not Ellen Francis, but Frances Ellen,' she began. 'In 1834 I was the prettiest young woman in Pontville, until –' She stopped and stared at the flames, her hands clasped on her lap.

'Go on,' someone finally whispered.

'The soldiers in their smart red uniforms used to march north to Launceston through our village, to the army barracks there. Our parents forbade us even to speak to them. But one day I caught the eye of a handsome cavalier named Henry, who arranged to meet me under the bridge. He brought me a bunch of violets, and we shared our first kiss.'

'Oooh,' Chad sighed. Ellen glared at him.

'When Henry and I parted, however, my father was standing waiting for me on the bridge, wielding a leather strap. I fled back along the narrow bridge – only a large wagon drawn by two horses was coming the other way. I pressed myself against the railing, as the wagon kept coming, coming . . .'

'And?'

'And I – was crushed by the side of the dray. I died instantly.'

There was total silence. 'So you came back as a ghost?' Miss Johns prompted.

'I was angry at having to leave this life. So I banged around the kitchen of my house at night, and stamped up the stairs, to disturb those who had been so hard on me. I come back often, to this day. Nobody sees me, but I leave behind the scent of those violets.'

'Amazing! 'I overheard Miss Johns saying later. 'You'd swear she believes her story.'

'Incredible imagination. Gave me the shivers,' agreed Gordon.

At bedtime the moon cast an eerie glow into our room. Ellen never spoke as we undressed, and I found myself wishing that I didn't have to share with someone so weird. Little did I know that my wish was about to come true!

'Your story was wicked,' I told her. 'I reckon you must really be a ghost!'

'I prayed no one would say that!!' she screeched. 'Did you have to spoil *everything*?'

Then, to my horror, she climbed on to the low sill – and flung herself out of the window.

'Ellen!!!' I screamed. I forced myself to look below. But to my amazement, there was no crumpled body. Instead, Ellen was running across the courtyard – and as I watched *she ran straight through the school bus* and down towards the lake.

My next scream woke the whole camp.

Miss Johns stayed with me all night, and Gordon has just been in. He has told everyone that I had a bad nightmare, and my parents are coming to get me. He had other news too.

'Pontville School says that Ellen Francis was a strange child, who came to believe that she was really Frances Ellen from long ago.'

'So she does exist!' I said, glancing at the costume lying on the other bed.

'Well, she did. One day last year she suddenly jumped up in class and cried, "Henry is waiting for me!" She dashed out of the yard towards the bridge – and was killed instantly by a truck.'

So here I am, wondering in a confused way whether my room-mate was one ghost or two. And as I think of her, the room is filling with the scent of violets.

The first of **ELIZABETH HUTCHINS'** many short stories was published over twenty years ago, and she has gone on to write picture books, novels for young people of all ages and most recently historical fiction. Her stories often feature places that she has visited; and so the setting for *The Scent of Violets* is the ghostly Struan House, near Naracoorte in South Australia, where she was once a leader at a camp for talented teenage writers. Like most authors, Elizabeth grabs hold of story ideas whenever they jump up at her, and jots them down. Her brain went into overdrive when she overheard a Tasmanian woman on an airport bus telling an American tourist about a ghost at her country home who rattled dishes and cutlery in the kitchen, stomped on the stairs – and always left behind the scent of violets . . .

FEDERICI IS NOT A CAT

EDEL WIGNELL

Willow hopped out of the bus and stood with her class and Mr Dan, their teacher, at the theatre entrance.

A guide came out. 'My name is Patrice,' she said. 'Welcome to the Princess Theatre. Some of you may be lucky enough to see Federici today.'

'Who's he?' Danny asked.

Patrice laughed. 'I'll tell you later.'

'Probably the theatre cat,' said Willow.

Everyone followed Patrice into the foyer. Willow looked about for Federici, the cat.

Patrice opened double-doors and took them into the theatre – a great space.

'Hundreds of seats!'

'Look at the lights!'

'Wow, the ceiling's high up!'

'Look at the balconies!'

'Hundreds more seats!'

The cat could be anywhere, thought Willow. Feeling

a strange presence, she shivered and looked around quickly. No one!

'Look on stage,' said Peta.

'For six months, we've been playing *The Phantom of the Opera*,' said Patrice. 'When it starts tonight, this is the first set the audience will see. Follow me – we'll go backstage.'

They followed along a corridor, up some steps, around a corner, past some dressing-rooms.

I mustn't get lost, Willow thought. I wouldn't be able to find my way out.

A cloaked figure appeared briefly, and she moved aside. It brushed past and disappeared through a half-open door. The cloak wafted a breeze around her legs.

'Was that a singer?' Willow asked, wide-eyed.

'There's no one here now,' said Patrice. 'Just us.'

'I didn't see anyone,' said Peta.

The class crammed into a dressing-room. Everyone grinned to friends in mirrors while Patrice told stories about famous singers.

Suddenly Willow smelt something burning. 'Toast!' she exclaimed. 'Turn off the toaster!'

Everyone laughed.

'Silly Willie,' said Peta. 'No one's making toast.'

Mr Dan frowned. 'Don't interrupt, please!'

Willow sniffed. I can smell it, for sure, she thought. If there's toast, there'll be a cat. She crouched and peered.

Patrice said, 'Follow me! This corridor is called Pneumonia Alley.'

Willow felt the breeze again, and the aroma of toast came more strongly. Someone's following me!

Patrice called, 'Time to go on stage.'

They walked around a great forest of scenery which would be wheeled on stage to change the scenes.

Everyone stood on stage and looked out into the great auditorium.

Mr Dan asked, 'How would it feel to sing with hundreds of people watching and listening.'

'Scary!'

'I promised to tell you about Federici,' said Patrice. 'Has anyone seen him yet?'

'Someone's here,' said Willow. 'I can feel someone, but I thought Federici would be a theatre cat.'

'No, not a cat, but you're right about a presence.'

Willow nodded and took a deep breath as the others looked at her.

Patrice continued. 'Federici was a great English singer. His real name was Frederick Baker, but his stage name was Francesco Federici.

'He came to Melbourne in 1888 to sing in an opera called *Faust*. He was supposed to play the part of the devil – called Mephistopheles. But, on the first night, something terrible happened.'

Patrice pointed. 'Here in the floor was a trap-door. When it was time for Mephistopheles to descend to hell, the trap-door opened and flames rose up. He had to step down through the flames into the basement, taking a man called Faust with him.'

Everyone breathed, 'Oooooh!'

'Mephistopheles wrapped his crimson cloak around Faust. The flames rose up. Then Mephistopheles collapsed with a heart attack. He was rushed off the stage, and a doctor came, but he died, aged thirty-eight.'

Patrice paused, and there was a hush. Everyone looked at the place where the trap-door had been, and imagined the scene.

Meanwhile, Willow felt eyes on her back. She turned around quickly, and looked up to the balcony. A man in evening dress sat in the front row. The studs on his white shirt-front glittered. She blinked, and he vanished.

'Now turn around,' said Patrice. 'Look up to the balcony. It's called the Dress Circle. These are the best seats. Some people have seen Federici sitting in the centre, staring at the empty stage.'

Willow wanted to say, 'I saw him,' but she knew that Mr Dan would say, 'Don't interrupt!'

Patrice continued. 'Stories have grown about Federici, our theatre ghost. Several singers have seen him: a wardrobe mistress, a fireman and a cleaner, too. Sometimes he takes a bow at the end of an opera.'

'Is he a friendly ghost?' Danny asked.

'Yes, I think so,' said Patrice. 'Some people say the Federici stories are nonsense, but there are people who have special psychic powers. They see and hear things that other people don't. Perhaps you have one in your class. Who smelt toast?'

'I did,' said Willow, and everyone stared. 'Someone brushed past in a corridor, and there was a breeze.'

'Yes,' said Patrice. 'Several people have felt the breeze of Federici's cloak, especially in the corridor called Pneumonia Alley. Other people have smelt toast there, too. Now, follow me to the balcony.'

She led the way along more corridors, up two marble staircases and across a foyer. They turned into the Dress Circle and sat in the front seats. Willow sat in the centre.

This is where Federici sat a few minutes ago, she thought. She stared at the stage and imagined Federici in his crimson cloak as Mephistopheles. The trapdoor opens, the flames rise, Mephistopheles descends . . .

Her skin crept and she shivered. When she looked around everyone had gone. Her heart thumped. She was lost! How could she get out? Quickly she ran up the aisle steps, through the door, across the foyer, down the marble staircase.

'This way, I think,' she puffed.

Another marble staircase led to the main foyer. Willow burst through the front door, onto the street

Mr Dan had been ticking names as the children hopped onto the bus. 'One missing! Where's Willow?'

Willow charged up the steps.

'Here I am!'

'We're starving!' shouted Danny.

'Next stop – a picnic in the gardens,' said Mr Dan.

If I'd stayed behind, Willow thought, I could've had toast with Federici!

EDEL WIGNELL is a freelance writer, compiler and journalist. She has been writing full time since 1979 for both adults and children, and has more than seventy published books to her name. Edel, who has five sisters, was born at Echuca in northern Victoria, Australia, and lived on a sheep farm for sixteen years. She taught in Victorian and London schools for eight years and at a teachers' college for seven. Interest in history, folklore and fantasy inspires much of Edel's writing and compiling, and family life is the common link in fiction, whether the stories are fantasy or reality. Edel lives with her husband Geoff in the foothills of the Dandenong Ranges east of Melbourne. For exercise Edel power-walks; she loves owls and is terrified of spiders!

DEAD OR ALIVE

JANEEN BRIAN

'If ye don't start,' Fergus McFinn warned his ancient utility truck one early, frosty morning, 'I'll give ye a boot up the exhaust!' The engine spluttered, whined at the chilliness of the day, and then started, burping out a cloud of black smoke.

'Good for you,' said Fergus and eased himself into the driver's seat. He backed back and swung the ute around. Then down he went. Down the slope of the rough driveway, still lined with dewy grass, and on to the road that led to the town of Beechmore.

He got a good park. Right outside the chemist. That pleased the old man. But before he switched off the ignition, he gave the car another stern warning. 'Remember what I tol' ye,' he said, as he rummaged for his prescription. 'It's a boot up the backside, if ye don't start.' He then walked into the shop.

'How are you, Fergus?' asked Caroline Pill, the chemist.

'I'm the same as that prescription,' said the old man. 'We both need replacing.'

Caroline smiled. 'And what about the ute? Is it behaving itself?' It was well known in the town that Fergus spoke to the car as he would a person.

'Cantankerous, as usual!' said Fergus and paid for his tablets.

'See you next week,' called Caroline.

'Mebbe,' Fergus muttered and walked back to the ute.

'A nice bloke,' said Caroline to her new assistant, Katie, 'but he won't make old bones.'

'What do you mean? Oh, I see,' nodded Katie. 'He's that sick, is he? Where does he live?'

'In an old house, about five k's out, on the side of a mountain. It's a lovely spot, but the place needs a bit of work now that Fergus can't do as much as he used to.'

'Mmm,' said Katie. 'Does he live alone, then?'

'Well, he's got Betsy,' said Caroline, with a secret smile.

'Oh,' said Katie. 'What's she like?'

Caroline laughed. 'An old wind-bag!'

At dusk, Fergus threw a tartan rug over the bonnet of the ute. 'That'll keep ye warm, ye fussy old thing. I don't want ye croakin' on me during the night.' And he went inside to get his dinner ready. Sausages and mash with a dollop of tomato sauce.

After washing his dishes, Fergus tapped the lid of the green teapot. 'Right, now! I'll set the kettle going, and then you can get all steamed up! I'll go and fetch Betsy.'

From the end of the dim hall, he called, 'I'm comin' me old dear.'

The bedroom door squeaked as he opened it. After switching on the light, Fergus walked up to the wooden chest that sat beneath the window. 'Ah,' he sighed, as he bent over. 'Come on. Up ye get.' And he lifted Betsy into his arms.

Back in the living room, the heater was warming to the idea of the evening's entertainment. The four bars glowed red and Fergus sat in a comfortable chair nearby. He was in no hurry. It always took a while to get Betsy going because of the amount of air she needed.

Once everything was ready, Fergus said, 'So, what will it be tonight, everyone: *Bonny Doon*, or *Scotland the Brave?*' He paused. A window rattled in the night breeze.

'Ah,' nodded Fergus, with a smile. '*Scotland the Brave*, it is then. Okay, Betsy?'

Fergus flicked the pipe into his mouth. He squeezed the tartan bag under his arm and his fingers played on the chanter. The melody from Betsy, Fergus's set of bagpipes, swelled and sang out. It seemed to march all around the room, as it had always done, night after night, in the old man's small mountain home.

When the clock struck ten, Fergus stood, his fingers stretching out to steady himself on the edge of the chair. He packed Betsy back into the box and settled down to sleep.

Outside a night thrush broke the icy silence.

◆

Days passed. The ute hadn't been seen around the place for a while. Soon it was common knowledge.

'I had a feeling,' sighed Caroline Pill to Katie, and ordered flowers for Fergus's funeral.

Betsy was buried with him.

◆

Caroline lived a short distance further on from Fergus's place. One warm evening, a few weeks later, she drove slowly towards it, her arm resting on the open window. She'd always liked the old man, for all his odd ways, and she wondered what was going to happen to the place now that he'd gone. But as the car was cruising close, Caroline heard an odd noise – a whining sound that strangely enough resembled bagpipes. Like *Betsy* when Fergus played her. But Betsy had been buried with Fergus. And the house was completely empty. At that moment, Caroline, sensible, level-headed Caroline, felt the skin of her scalp lift and tighten. Hastily, she checked her rear-view mirror, put the car into gear and pressed her foot on the accelerator.

Soon Caroline's story became common knowledge. Other townsfolk drove up the road – and returned, puzzled, and ready to spread the word. But when the real estate agent went to knock in the FOR SALE sign, he vouched again for the emptiness of the place. He was somewhat pale, too, as he vouched.

Around town, no one spoke any longer of Fergus's place, without adding the word that had spread.

Ghost.

Before the auction, Katie from the chemist's decided it was time that she found out more about the countryside in which she now lived. She loved hiking. She loved birds. And she loved photography. So, one Sunday afternoon, she set off with her camera and supplies in her backpack.

It was a great day for hiking, warm but not too hot and everything around seemed fresh and alive: the air, the birds' songs, the wildflowers. Without realising it, Katie had come upon the road to Fergus's place. She read the details on the sign and then looked towards the house, at the end of the slope. There was no strange sound, but even so, she glanced from side to side before heading up the driveway.

The house was small and weathered and surrounded by overgrown bushes and trees. As she drew closer, Katie stepped into the shadows of tall trees. The air grew chill and made her shiver. By now she'd reached the small porch at one side. She stepped towards the front door, when a sound screeched through the air.

Katie froze. Eyes wide, she slowly turned her head. The sound faltered then began again. Again the tune faltered, and then changed. Katie gripped a porch pole to steady herself. She turned to run. But her feet stood still, as though they were pinned to the ground.

Then something hammered in her brain. It banged for recognition. It was not the fear. It was the tune. The *tune*. Why did she know it? Why was it so familiar? Of course! It was an old Scottish song that her mother had sung to her. It was *Scotland the Brave*.

Then, suddenly, as Katie was getting her breath back ready to head down the slope, it stopped. The only noise then was a scuffle, a scampering – there, in the bushes.

Katie McPherson, the ever-ready photographer, raised her camera and clicked.

It wouldn't be a perfect shot.

But you couldn't expect a perfect shot from a lyrebird as it dashed for cover. Fast-moving, shy lyrebird – natural mimic of the bush.

As she continued her way down the slope, Katie Ferguson smiled wryly and said, 'I wonder if it can do *Bonny Doon* as well?'

JANEEN BRIAN, an ex-teacher and actor, has been writing for over 25 years, 14 of those full-time. Many of her 60 children's books have won awards or been translated, and she writes across the genres because that interests and challenges her: picture books, short fiction, non-fiction and poetry, magazine articles and plays. Her popular picture book, *Where does Thursday go?* and her non-fiction book, *Pilawuk – When I was Young* were both Honour Books in the CBC Awards, while many others, such as *Dog Star*, and *Leaves for Mr Walter*, were Notable Books.

30 AUSTRALIAN GHOST STORIES FOR CHILDREN

THE EXORCIST'S CLUB

Excerpt from *Eloise*
CATHERINE JINKS

Playing about with ghosts can be dangerous. That's why I wasn't too keen on the Exorcist's Club. But when Michelle begged me, I gave in. How could I have known that the séance would be such a disaster?

It was all Michelle's fault. I never wanted to summon up spirits of the dead. I wouldn't have tried, if it hadn't been for the Exorcist's Club. And the Exorcist's Club was Michelle's idea.

'The Exorcist's Club?' I said doubtfully, when she first made the suggestion. 'What would that be for?'

'What do you think?' she replied. 'We'd go around getting rid of ghosts. *Exorcising* ghosts. For money.'

I stared at her. We were in the school library – as we generally are, at lunchtime. (We have to be, because we're library monitors, now.) And of course we weren't really supposed to be chatting away, though Mrs Proctor doesn't mind a bit of noise as long as we keep our voices down and do our jobs. My job is putting books away. Michelle's job is looking after the computers. When no one's having trouble with the internet, or doing stupid things with a mouse pad, Michelle usually helps me.

She's my best friend, but that doesn't mean we always agree on everything.

'What makes you think we can get rid of ghosts?' I asked and she clicked her tongue.

'You got rid of Eglantine, didn't you?' she said, as she shoved a copy of *The Silver Chair* firmly between *The Last Battle* and *The Voyage of the Dawn Treader*. 'Your house was haunted, and you got rid of the ghost. Not to mention that business at Hill End – '

'Yes, but hang on a minute.' I needed time to think. 'You told me once that you saw a film with an exorcist in it, and the exorcist was a priest.'

'I didn't see it. My cousin saw it.'

'Whatever.' I waved a book at her. 'My point is, the exorcist in that film was fighting a demon, wasn't he? It threw people out windows, and twisted their heads around, and made them speak in strange, spooky voices. That's what you said, isn't it?'

'Yes, but – '

'Eglantine didn't do any of those things. And we didn't *exorcise* her. You have to use prayers and things to exorcise things. Rituals.'

'No, you don't.'

'Yes, you do. I read it in a dictionary.'

So we went to look at *The Shorter Oxford English Dictionary*, which no one ever uses at out school – it's disgraceful. Sure enough, the first definition of 'exorcise' was 'to drive out (an evil spirit) by the use of a holy name'.

'See?' I said. 'A holy name. I don't know how to do that, I wouldn't even want to.'

'Yes, but look at the second definition.' Michelle's forefinger stabbed at another line of print. "To clear of evil spirits; to purify". There's nothing about holy names or rituals.'

'Eglantine wasn't an evil spirit. She was confused. As soon as we finished the story she was trying to write, she disappeared.'

'Allie.' Michelle was getting impatient. 'That isn't the point.'

'Shh!' I warned, with a quick glance at Mrs Procter's office. Obediently, Michelle lowered her voice.

'The point is, you're an expert, now,' she hissed. 'You know more about ghosts than practically anybody. So why not start a club?'

'Because I don't want to.' I'm not a clubby sort of person, you see. I'm not a joiner. But then Michelle cocked her head, and fixed me with a penetrating look.

'Peter wants to,' she said,

'Peter Cresciani?'

'Yup.'

'Oh.'

That made me pause. Don't get the wrong idea – it's not as if I have a crush on Peter, or anything. It's just that he's a friend of mine, and very intelligent, and if he thinks that something is a good idea, then it's worth considering.

'You've talked to him about this?' I inquired, and Michelle nodded. 'What did he say?'

'He said he'd be interested in joining.'

'Really?'

'But only if you're in it.'

'When did he say that?'

'This morning. At recess.'

I had been chasing up lost property at recess: my brother's lost property, to be exact. Bethan never remembers to ask at the office when he's mislaid a hat or a drink bottle, so Mum makes me do it.

That lost-property box practically has his name on it.

'Well . . . I don't know,' I said. 'People already think I'm weird.'

'No, they don't.'

'Yes, they do.' People always think you're weird when you read lots of books, and keep a collection of animal skulls in your bedroom. A reputation for seeing ghosts only makes things worse. 'Is this going to be a *secret* club? I could handle a secret club.'

'Don't be silly. What would be the point of a secret club? We want people to contact us if they have any ghost problems.'

'People like who?'

'I don't know. Anybody.'

'People at school?'

'Perhaps. Or other people.'

I hesitated.

'It would just be us three,' Michelle went on. 'You, me and Peter. Most of it would be historical research. The way you did with Eglantine. Death certificates and stuff.'

'But we don't have any equipment,' I protested. When my family was trying to get rid of Eglantine, we used an organisation called PRISM (which stands for Paranormal Research Investigation Services and Monitoring). The PRISM people had brought to our house lots of different equipment: Geiger counters, electromagnetic field detectors, infra-red cameras. 'You need special equipment to detect the presence of a ghost.'

'Yes, but not for getting rid of a ghost. You got rid of Eglantine by working out what she wanted, and you did that by working out who she was.'

Michelle was right. I couldn't deny it. And I must

admit that I had liked researching Eglantine's background. I'm one of those people who likes research projects. I can't help it. With a research project you get to play detective, only you're hunting down clues in libraries and on databases, instead of following footprints or getaway cars.

'We-e-ell . . .' I said.

'Come on Allie. Please?' Michelle put on her fawning puppy act, panting and pressing her hands together at the wrist, like paws. It always annoys me – as she knows quite well. 'Pretty please?'

'Oh, stop.'

'*Please*, Allie?'

'All right, all right! I'll do it!'

CATHERINE JINKS was born in Brisbane in 1963 and grew up in Sydney and Papua New Guinea. She studied medieval history at university, and her love of reading led her to become a writer. She lives in the Blue Mountains in New South Wales with her Canadian husband and her daughter, Hannah. She has written over 20 books for children and adults, including the award-winning *Pagan* series.

THE SMELL OF GOAT

Excerpt from *The Binna Binna Man*
MEME MCDONALD AND BOORI MONTY PRYOR

In Binna Binna country you should watch where you go, even on a night when life is so stuffed up that nothing matters any more. You go wandering too far and you might come face to face with your worst nightmare – the Binna Binna man.

There's a hairyman up there, up at Yarrie. The Binna Binna man. That's what they call that eunjee, that spirit. He's a big fulla. Stinks real bad, like a goat. My cousin's uncle reckons you hear a chain rattling when he's coming for you. And if he comes for you, he gets you.

That's where we're going now, Yarrie. Migaloo fullas, whitefullas, call Yarrie a reserve or a mission or something. We just call it our place. That's where my mum's people come from. They tell you stories about that hairyman, that Binna Binna man, make you wish there was no night.

He's called the Binna Binna man 'cause he's got big

long ears. Binna means ears, see. He's got ears that long they drag on the ground, true. Drag along the ground as he walks.

The old people call those spirits Quinkins. They reckon the Binna Binna man can be good and heal you and stuff. But you poke fun at him or go to touch him when he don't want to be touched, then you can get into big trouble, like die.

We're in Binna Binna country now. Mountains full of bush, clouds hanging low, rolling down to the sea. The road winds round then takes off up the last big hill. Once we're over this one, we're there.

Trees come crowding in, tall and dark. Babe's headlights tunnel us through. I draw in a deep breath of that damp mountain air. We're climbing up slowly. No way I want to break down now. We all lean forward, trying to help Babe up. I reckon even Popeye don't want to be walking round in the dark out here.

There was a whitefulla once. He didn't believe in the Binna Binna man. He was always laughing at us Murris, saying we were crazy. Anyway, he was driving his ute up this hill. Must've been this same one. It was a real dark night. He came round that corner up there and he seen the Binna Binna man standing in the middle of the road. Huge and hairy, big long ears, pointy like Martians'. That ugly you gotta look away. The whitefulla swerved and skidded. The ute ended up hanging over the cliff there. He couldn't get out 'cause the car would have tipped and gone crashing over the edge.

He's clinging onto the steering wheel, waiting to die. That Binna Binna man come over and lifted his ute up, back onto the road. He give him a push start. That bloke took off like a mad thing. Never come out to Yarrie again.

Not at night. Never even goes outside his own house after dark no more.

I didn't think I'd ever cry again. Not after looking down into that dead hole, that grave, with my cus' that I loved lying there. But I can't go any further. I'm worn out. And I'm crying and I'm falling over.

'You're running away.' I hear a voice, real faint, from a long way off. 'Shut up!' I'm trying to yell out but really I know that long-way-off place is inside me. I block my ears even harder. I'm not listening. Same time I'm aching for that sweet voice to keep talking. There's a war broken out in me.

I fall flat on my face. I'm sobbing all right. And I'm hitting out, striking at anything. I'm losing. That fire in me is burning out. Everything hurts. My face from falling, my arms from hitting, my heart from breaking, and my mouth 'cause it's stuffed full of sand. If I keep crying, I'll choke. If I don't, I'll die. I give up, I give in.

A scream rips through the dark. Shandell. I gotta move. I gotta help her. I can't. Nothing works.

I can hear something clanging, like chains. A smell gets up my nose that sucks the breath right out of me. I don't know what goats smell like, but this is like nothing on earth. I can't get away. My legs and arms have sunk into the sand.

This hand touching me is moist and soft like a cloud slopped down off the mountain, wrapping round. And that breath, close to my ear, is warm, He's breathing for me, in and out. I keep my eyes shut.

The Binna Binna man's voice rumbles like thunder. I can hear him, but. 'You listen, boy. You open your ears and you listen. You been given things. The old people, your ancestors, been looking after you. You turn your back on them, you die. Now you listen.'

They're both talking to me now – that grumbly, old voice of the Binna Binna man and that clear voice I know so well, that sweet voice, deep inside, that I been blocking out. 'There's nowhere to run. You can't hide from yourself.' That's her voice, my girragundji, that's me.

That Binna Binna man's still there, making me listen. 'Be who you are.'

MEME McDONALD grew up in western Queensland and now lives in Melbourne. She is an award-winning author of books for adults and younger readers. She has published eight books, five of which have been written in collaboration with Aboriginal writer and storyteller and performer Boori Monty Pryor. Visit Meme's website at www.mememcdonald.com

BOORI MONTY PRYOR is Kunggandji and Birri-gubba from north Queensland. He is a writer and performer who, together with Meme McDonald, has written five award-winning books: *Maybe Tomorrow, My Girragundji, The Binna Binna Man, Njanjul the Sun* and *Flytrap*. He regularly performs for school students and adults around Australia and overseas.

A WET, MAGIC NIGHT

Excerpt from *The Nargun and the Stars*
PATRICIA WRIGHTSON

The Nargun was as old as the earth itself. When it began to move, it dragged its stony weight across 800 miles and 100 years, sometimes quietly and in peace, sometimes in sudden savage anger. Now it was in Wongadilla, in the Hunter Valley. Here Simon Brent came to know the spirits of the swamps and the mountains: the Potkoorok with its tricks; the Turongs, wreaking havoc with the road workers' equipment; the Nyols rustling and whispering in the rocks. In Wongadilla he first encountered the Nargun . . . and its frightening power.

[Simon] sat up again. If he could hear that, then the rain must be stopping. He couldn't have heard it ten minutes ago. He eased the window up again and put his head out.

Black shapes of trees sprang up and vanished. Thunder scolded. The rain was quite light when you heard it on the grass instead of on the roof. There were stars again, wide fields of them between the black flying clouds. It was still windy out there, but down here there were only gusts to shake splattering showers out of the trees... There was moonlight! The air was so clear that wetness had a cold white shine from the moonlight... There were black shadows flying, bigger than birds...

The black shadows were leaping from tree to tree, from high to low. Arms and legs were spread, straggling beards floated. They called each other in high, wild voices above and around the house. Excitement ran prickling along Simon's veins. He tumbled silently out of bed, rolled up his pyjama-legs, pulled on shorts and a raincoat and tennis shoes, climbed out of the window, and closed it down except for a space where he could fit his fingers. He was outside in the wet moonlight with black shadows leaping and calling overhead.

He went quietly towards the shed, and when he was nearer that than the house spoke softly to the dogs. Just as well he had been helping Charlie feed them; they only whimpered a bit when he told them to be quiet, and then he was past.

His shoes were wet and clammy-cold already. The rain had stopped, but the trees shook down drops that rattled on his raincoat and freckled his face with cold. The storm flashed and rumbled farther away, but here were only the calls of the flitting shadows and the water-noises – the *cluck* and *chinkle* of the creek down there in the gully; the louder rush and babble of the river; the quiet mutter of water running over the ground and sopping into his shoes, and somewhere the singing of water over high rocks.

Simon went running through the wet, shining white world, up the ridge past the head of the gully and then west to the swamp – seeing brambles and rocks and logs just in time to jump over them or swerve aside – somehow never falling – lifted and hurried along by the wet magic night. He went running right into the swamp before he heard another sound than water-noises, and then he stopped, up to his ankles in the swamp. The song of frogs went creaking and hiccupping up to the moon, and beyond the swamp was a clank and rattle of metal.

The road came out of a blackness of trees, water running down in a sheet because the mountain poured it off too fast for the gutters to carry it away. Into the moonlight came the grader as if the water carried it, clanking along slow and majestic like a lanky skeleton ship. But all round it there was a flurry of shadows, calling and crying as they had in the trees. Wispy arms waved, stick-like knees bent, shadowy beards tossed. They crowded the cabin and rode on the blade and clustered along its sides, the Turongs carrying the grader.

The boy stared, breathing hard. When the grader reached the turn it left the road and came on down to the swamp, slow and majestic like a battleship, but clanking as it was carried along by the crowd of dancing shadows. More of them came down from the trees, calling in windy voices. The grader reached the deep end of the swamp, and there the Potkoorok was waiting.

Into the shallows while frogs were shrieking; on while the wheels sank deeper and the blade dipped under. A lurch, a slow roll, a sinking down of the cabin roof; dark water heaving under the moon – the grader was gone. The Turongs rustled and stamped and jigged, the Potkoorok leapt and chuckled. The boy ran away, slopping through the swamp while the frogs shrieked.

He wanted to yell with delight or terror. He wanted to dance with the stamping, jigging, hopping crowd – if only he hadn't dreaded that they might come near. There was nothing to do but run. He splashed through runnels and stumbled over bushes while the cries died away behind. The wet magic night no longer held him up, and once he fell over. That made him realise that the moon was now hidden and he was running in the dark. A few last rags of cloud had blown across just as he left the swamp.

He would have to stop being stupid. He stood still and listened to the watery night. He remembered he should be walking across a gradual slope with a steep rise on the right and the ridge running down to the left. The easier slope of the ridge should guide him to the house, even if the moon didn't come out again soon – and it would, of course. It wasn't even dark, now that he looked, except for the close-looming blackness of the mountain. In the grey light of stars and cloudy moon he could see darker shapes ahead.

He squelched on. A faint grey shine was the wet wood of a fallen branch; he walked carefully around it. There was a tree close by in the blackness of the hillside. He felt its closeness, and found it by putting out a hand and touching wet bark. Branches stirred, and drops pelted on his raincoat. The darkness and slow groping made him colder.

Something moved; he felt it close to him. Invisible against the mountain something big and solid moved a little. Simon stood still and listened: no snort from Pet, no breathing, no twitch of ear or tail. He listened as he had not known he could, listened with every inch of his skin: he heard nothing. No pumping heart, no quietly streaming blood. Only the unhearable sound of earth taking a weight, only the universe shifting to balance a small movement. He wanted to put out a hand to discover what moved close by – but the dark places in his mind told his hand to be still as they told his heart to beat quietly.

The moon's edge lifted from the cloud; there was a soft polished light, and he saw a crooked shape. About a yard away – leaning forward – a hard, craggy, blunt-muzzled head and the smallest, most secret movement of a limb. Something without heart or blood, the living earth in a squat and solid shape, reached very secretly, a very little, for Simon.

PATRICIA WRIGHTSON was born in Lismore, New South Wales, the daughter of a country solicitor. One of a family of six, she lived in some fairly remote places and her schools ranged from a two-teacher school to a year of boarding in Queensland. Patricia is one of Australia's most distinguished writers for children. Since 1956 when her first novel *The Crooked Snake* was published, she has won many prestigious awards all over the world including an OBE in 1977, the Dromkeen Medal in 1984 and the Hans Christian Andersen Medal in 1986, all for her services to children's literature. Many of her books have been shortlisted for the Children's Book of the Year Award, which she has won four times for *The Crooked Snake*, *The Nargun and the Stars*, *The Ice Is Coming* and *A Little Fear*. Patricia's latest books include the Aussie Bites *Rattler's Place*, *The Sugar Gum Tree* and *The Water-dragons*, all illustrated by David Cox.

THE WHITE BULL

From *Shudders and Shakes*
ANNE INGRAM
(retold from various sources)

This story was recorded in the police files as well as being retold in his reminiscences by one of the police officers who took part in this strange and ghostly happening.

The year 1876 was very dry, there had been no rain for several months and the area around Queanbeyan in New South Wales was beginning to feel the effects — water was low, stock was being moved, and everyone talked about drought.

On the banks of the Murrumbidgee River, near an area called the Washpen, lived a shepherd. He worked for a Mr Davis and was responsible for the sheep and cattle in that particular area of the property.

On June 28 the police at Queanbeyan received a report that the shepherd had been found dead near his log cabin and that murder was suspected. The police rode out to the cabin, collected their evidence then buried the body, first wrapping it in a blanket which they found in the cabin.

Some weeks later a local identity was caught and charged with the murder of the shepherd. When the police began to assemble their case they realised that one vital piece of evidence was missing: the old blanket they had used to wrap the body in before burial. A police party of four men was then dispatched to collect the blanket.

They rode out to the Washpen one afternoon with their picks and shovels, arriving about two o'clock on a beautifully clear day. The sun shone strongly on their backs as the men began their task. Suddenly, as the first pick hit the soil, a huge, dark, threatening cloud appeared from nowhere and locked the area in darkness.

With a slight shiver the men continued with their unpleasant task. Then, as the spade of one of the men hit the log which was covering the body, a tremendous explosion shattered the air and echoed around the surrounding hills. The ground trembled and seemed to sink beneath their feet while, from the hills behind, came the sound of thunderous hoofbeats.

As the four stunned men stood looking through the gloom which surrounded them, a large white bull materialised on the side of the closest hill and came charging straight towards the men. Without a second's hesitation the men grabbed their tools and headed for the safety of the trees further back. Here they waited and watched in trembling silence as the giant animal came rushing on at a speed which seemed incredible for his size and weight.

This great white bull looked neither to left nor right, only towards the open grave of the shepherd. He thundered towards it but stopped, suddenly, right at its edge. Here he stood for a few moments, head high, then slowly, with a moaning sound coming from deep within his throat, the white bull began to paw the ground. He kept this up for about five minutes then he lay down beside the open grave and with one last, long sigh he died.

It took the men several minutes to realise just what had happened. White and very shaky, they came towards the animal. Each man in turn checked to make sure that the bull was really dead, then without wasting a minute they collected the blanket and headed for home.

The next day extensive enquiries were made throughout the district to find the owner of this magnificent white bull. No one came to claim it, neither did anyone know of such an animal anywhere round the area.

Once again the four men set out for the Washpen, this time to bury the white bull. When they arrived at the scene there was no sign of the animal nor was there any trace of it ever having been there.

THE BLACK HORSE OF SUTTON

From *Shudders and Shakes*
ANNE INGRAM
(retold from various sources)

The Monaro district of New South Wales is well served with ghosts and one of the most interesting stories to come from here concerns a phantom black horse whose appearance to a family always foretells the death of one of the household.

The first appearance, early last century, of the Black Horse of Sutton was to the wife of the owner of a property in the Monaro district. One mild summer's night she was sitting on the verandah of the homestead waiting for her husband to return from a business trip to Goulburn, where he had gone that morning to arrange for the purchase of some land to extend his holding.

As he was riding home he was thrown from his horse and killed instantly. His wife, waiting quietly on the verandah, heard the faint sound of galloping hoofs along the dusty road. There was silence, then she heard the gate open and the turning of a horse as though the rider had closed the gate. And again the galloping of hoofs along the road.

The woman rose and went forward ready to welcome her husband. She was puzzled because he had not cooeed as he usually did when he reached the home paddock. As she stood waiting a riderless horse came into view. It was not her husband's horse, neither was it a horse which belonged to the property. This strange horse was jet black.

The horse came on at full gallop. It crossed the front lawn at breakneck speed coming straight towards the house. The horse had passed straight through the house. The woman stood transfixed as the sound of galloping echoed from the ranges beyond.

She waited all that night for her husband to return trying to fight down the fear which was rising inside her. She hoped it had all been a trick of her imagination but somehow she knew there was something wrong. Next day her husband's body was found, and nearby his horse was quietly grazing.

The riderless black horse was to make two more appearances to this family – he became their messenger of death. During the Boer War this same woman's eldest son was killed and later she was to lose her youngest son in an accident. On both occasions the news of the death was preceded by the strange and terrifying gallop of the Black Horse of Sutton.

ANNE INGRAM was born in 1937 in Manilla, New South Wales. As one of Australia's best-known editors and publishers, she has been responsible for establishing the careers of many authors and illustrators. She was the first Australian publisher to represent her country at the Bologna Children's Book Fair where she introduced Australian children's books to the world. In 1984 Anne won the Lady Cutler Award and in 1985 the Dromkeen Medal in recognition for her services to Australian Children's Literature. In

1988 Anne established the publishing house Anne Ingram Books in association with William Collins. She also has a winning writing partnership with Peggy O'Donnell, an ex-teacher, and the two have produced many best-selling educational and non-fiction books, such as *Money! Money!*, *The Great Indoors* and *My Money, Myself*, a hands-on financial guide especially tailored for women. Anne has also edited many collections and compilations of stories, including *The Pickled Boeing* and *Shudders and Shakes*, and written illustrated book texts, such as *Making a Picture Book* with Bob Graham and *Run Damon, Run!* with Junko Morimoto. She lives in Sydney and takes pleasure in gardening and rearing a rare species of frog.

THE LITTLE FURRY GIRL

Excerpt from *Playing Beatie Bow*
RUTH PARK

The game is called Beatie Bow and the children play it for the thrill of scaring themselves. But when Abigail is drawn in, the game is quickly transformed into an extraordinary, sometimes horrifying, adventure as she finds herself transported to a place that is foreign yet strangely familiar . . .

After Abigail's father had gone away, Kathy [her mother] had given a last decisive sniff, washed her face, which was somewhat like that of a fat-cheeked finch with a finch's shiny dewdrop eyes, raked her hair up on top of her head in a washerwoman's knot, and rented a black hole of Calcutta in a Paddington lane. This she turned into a treasure-house of trendy trivia. She called the shop Magpies, and soon other magpie people flocked around to shriek and snatch and buy.

What with Kathy being a success, and Grandmother getting more interested in Bridge and less of a carper, Abigail and her mother achieved a kind of happiness.

Now she jumped up with a scowl, banged the door on the empty place, and went visit the Crowns, her neighbours.

That unit was in its customary state of theatrically awful mess. Justine Crown didn't believe in housework. She said the children came first: but she hadn't made a gold-medal job of them either. Usually Natalie, the four-year-old, was at kindergarten, and Vincent, the high-rise monster at school. But as it was holidays they were both home, and Vincent, who was in Abigail's opinion the grimmest kid two agreeable people could be cursed with, was at his usual game of worrying Natalie like a dog with a bone.

Natalie aroused in Abigail a solemnly protective feeling. This rather embarrassed her. The little girl was prone to sudden fevers, nightmares, fears, and a kind of helpless affection for the frightful Vincent that did not allow her to defend herself against him.

Vincent was a bundle of bones with a puzzling smell, as though he'd wet himself six weeks earlier and not bothered to bathe. He was as sharp as a knife and had his parents sized up to the last millimetre. Abigail did not see that his face was wretched as well as cunning, and she was sincerely flattered that he hated her more than he hated anyone else.

'You've got Dracula teeth,' he greeted her.

Justine shouted from the kitchen, 'Oh, for heaven's sake don't start on Abigail, you little beast.' She came out, bashing around in a basin with a fork. 'He's been in a dark blue hell all day.'

'Dracula teeth,' said Vincent. 'Big long white choppers. See them, Fat Nat?'

'Don't call your sister that, and if Abigail's teeth are too big it's because her face hasn't grown up to them yet.'

Instantly Abigail imagined herself with this thin nosy face and fangs sticking out over her lower lip.

She was very depressed with her looks as it was, and had given up hope of developing fascinating high cheekbones or eyelashes an inch long. She liked her eyebrows, which were black and straight, and her long brown hair, which glistened satisfactorily. But although her mother assured her that her figure would arrive some day, she often despaired. Most times people took her for twelve, which was humiliating.

However, she was not going to be bugged by any six-year-old dinosaur like Vincent Crown. She glared at him.

'Knock off the wisecracks!' To Justine she said, 'It's freezing outside, but would you like me to take them down to the playground till it starts to get dark?'

The noise [in the playground] was shattering. Most of the children came from Mitchell [their tower block], but others probably lived in the cottages round about. Abigail observed that those racing dementedly back and forth performed their charges in a certain order. They were playing a group game.

'Would you like to play it, too, Natty?'

Natalie shook her head. Her big grey eyes were now full of tears. Abigail sighed. Justine was for ever trailing Natalie off to a doctor who was supposed to be miraculous with highly strung children, but he hadn't brought off any miracles yet.

'Now what's the matter, little dopey?'

'They're playing Beatie Bow and it scares me. But I like to watch. Please let's watch,' pleaded Natalie.

'Never heard of it,' said Abigail. She noticed Vincent rushing to join in and thought how weird it was that in the few years that had passed since she was six or seven the kids had begun to play such different games. She watched this one just in case Vincent murdered anyone. She could already hear him squealing like a mad rat.

Natalie took hold of a fistful of her shawl, and Abigail held her close to keep her out of the wind. The child was shivering. Yet the game didn't look so exciting; just one more goofy kid's game.

First of all the children formed a circle. They had become very quiet. In the middle was a girl who had been chosen by some counting-out rhyme.

'That's Mudda,' explained Natalie.

'What's Mudda?'

'You know, a mummy like my mummy.'

'Oh, Mother!'

'Yes, she's called Mudda. That's in the game.'

Someone hidden behind the concrete pipes made a scraping sound. The children chorused, 'Oh, Mudda, what's that?'

'Nothing at all,' chanted the girl in the centre. 'The dog at the door, the dog at the door.'

Now a bloodcurdling moan was heard from behind the pipes. Abigail felt Natalie press closer to her. She noticed that the dark was coming down fast; soon it would rain. She resolved she would take the children home as soon as she could gather up Vincent.

'Oh, Mudda, what's that, what can it be?'

'The wind in the chimney, that's all, that's all.'

There was a clatter of stones being dropped. Some of the younger children squawked, and were hushed.

'Oh, Mudda, what's that, what's that, can you see?'

'It's the cow in the byre, the horse in the stall.'

Natalie held on tightly and put her hands over her eyes.

'Don't look, Abigail, it's worse than awful things on TV!'

At this point Mudda pointed dramatically beyond the circle of children. A girl covered in a white sheet or tablecloth was creeping towards them, waving her arms and wailing.

'It's Beatie Bow,' shrieked Mudda in a voice of horror, 'risen from the dead!'

At this the circle broke and the children ran shrieking hysterically to fling themselves in a chaotic huddle of arms and legs in the sandpit at the other end.

'What on earth was all that about?' asked Abigail. She felt cold and grumpy and made gestures at Vince to rejoin them.

'The person who is Beatie Bow is a ghost, you see,' explained Natalie, 'and she rises from her grave, and everyone runs and pretends to be afraid. If she catches someone, that one has to be the next Beatie Bow. But mostly the children *are* frightened, because they play it and play it till it's dark. Vincent gets in a state and that's why he's so mean afterwards. But the little furry girl doesn't get scared,' she added inconsequentially. 'I think she'd like to join in, she smiles so much. Look, Abigail, see her watching over there?'

Before the older girl could look, Vincent panted up, scowling.

'We're going to play it again! I want to! I want to!'

'No way,' said Abigail firmly. 'It's getting dark and it's too cold for Natalie already.'

The boy said bitterly, 'I hate you!'

'Big deal,' said Abigail.

Vincent pinched Natalie cruelly. Tears filled her eyes. 'You see? Just like I told you,' she said without rancour.

'What a creep you are, Vincent,' said Abigail scornfully.

Vincent made a rude gesture and ran on before them

into the lobby. As they waited for the lift, Abigail saw that his whole body was trembling. She made up her mind to have a word with Justine about the too-exciting game.

'I saw the little furry girl, Vince,' said Natalie. 'She was watching you again.'

He ignored her, barged past them into the Crown unit, and flung himself down before the TV.

RUTH PARK was born in Auckland, New Zealand, in 1922. She moved to Australia in 1942 and married the writer D'Arcy Niland. After their marriage the Nilands travelled through outback Australia, working in a variety of jobs, from shearer's cook to fruit packer, before settling down in Surry Hills in Sydney, where they earned a living writing full-time. Ruth has written over fifty books for both children and adults and has won many prizes, including the prestigious Miles Franklin Award for her novel *Swords and Crowns and Rings* (1977), and *Playing Beatie Bow* was winner of the 1981 Children's Book Council of Australia Book of the Year Award and the 1984 Boston Globe Award. In 1993 she was awarded the Lloyd O'Neil Magpie Award for services to the Australian book industry.

INVISIBLE TEA

Excerpt from *The Ghost of Love Street*
VENERO ARMANNO

Sam is a skateboarder with a heart full of pain. He desperately misses Samantha, his beautiful girlfriend, who is no longer in this world. Or is she? On the anniversary of her murder, when Sam visits her old house in Love Street, does he really expect to find her again? Will he give her that final kiss he's dreamed about and set them both free?

It was such a weird relief to see Samantha Yen-Khe again. Sam wiped away his tears. She was waiting for him inside the old and musty, falling-down Yen-Khe family home.

Sam had come in through the back of the house. The windows over the kitchen were long-since broken and boarded up, but it took nothing to pull the splintery old wood away and make an aperture he could climb through. Sam had avoided walking up Love Street, where anyone would have seen him and maybe recognised him. Instead he'd passed through many backyards of weeds and long green grass, with their bent Hills Hoists and old snoozing dogs too lazy to bark at a slowly creeping boy.

So now, here was Samantha.

She was sitting on an old three-legged wooden chair in what used to be the living room. Sam remembered very well what the whole house used to be like when he'd been a frequent visitor here. He especially remembered the living room, where all the colourful furniture and knick-knacks that Mrs Yen-Khe liked to arrange and rearrange always made him feel at home. None of Mrs Yen-Khe's things were left any more. The walls used to be covered with photographs of family in Vietnam, of the Yen-Khes' wedding day, of the Yen-Khe restaurant in the West End. Mostly, too, there had been photos of their daughter Samantha.

Now those walls were bare, with holes in the peeling wallpaper.

But as if nothing had ever happened and she was a normal fourteen-year-old girl sitting in her family home, Samantha was there in the empty cobwebby, thoroughly gloomy room. A shimmery sort of light etched a shadow around her. Samantha was there all right, but she seemed lighter than air, as if a gust of breeze through the floor timbers or from the tumbling-down ceiling would blow her away.

Samantha turned.

Sam saw how serene and pretty she was. Her hair was long, jet-black, lustrous, and her cheekbones were high. She was just the way Sam remembered, her lips curled in that half-smile he had never forgotten.

Sam thought, Boy have I gone out of my mind. It's finally happened. I've gone totally loony. He rubbed his eyes very, very hard.

Samantha said, 'Well, finally, there you are, Sam. Where have you been?'

'I . . . I . . .,' was all he could get out of his frozen-tight throat.

'I've been waiting here forever, Sammy. Don't you remember what we were going to do?'

Sam used every last bit of will power to find his voice. He said, 'I had to go to school. I just couldn't get away.'

'School? You went to school on a Saturday?'

'It's not Saturday.'

Samantha gave him a look, her nose crinkling playfully as if he was pulling a joke on her. The three-legged chair she sat upon was perfectly balanced. It should have been falling over, but Samantha floated there, nice and relaxed.

'I think we're too late now,' she said. 'We've missed the start of the movie. Well, we don't really have to go anywhere, do we? Mum and Dad are at the restaurant. We've got the place to ourselves.'

Samantha stood up and Sam couldn't help but take a step back.

The way she now moved around the dank and empty room was a lot like gliding. Sam's heart thudded. He'd flown down the rain-filled streets to get there and Samantha glided around a dead old room. We're a perfect match, Sam thought, except that she's deceased and I'm not.

Now Samantha was making strange movements.

He said, 'What are you doing?'

Samantha continued a mime he didn't understand. She said, 'Putting some music on, what does it look like I'm doing? This one's for you.'

Sam understood it now, even if he couldn't see it. She *was* putting music on. It was a record, one of those old vinyl records Samantha used to love better than compact discs. Her hands moved in space, putting the record onto the turntable, lowering the needle, adjusting the volume. Nothing was there of course, except for Samantha, etched in white light.

Sam thought he would lose consciousness.

'Now. Like it?' Samantha asked.

A bit trembly in the knees Sam replied, 'Well, what is it?'

'It's your favourite. Sammy, you're being very strange today.'

There wasn't a thing to hear. There was no music at all. Utter silence enveloped the battered old house. Maybe Sam hadn't even heard Samantha's voice. Maybe he was imagining everything. Maybe he was dead himself, and that was why he could see Samantha Yen-Khe again. A car could have hit him on the way there, or he'd fallen under the wheels of one of those suburban trains.

Sam listened hard. There was nothing, but a thought did occur to him.

'The Beatles. It's the Beatles.'

'Of course it is.'

Sam and Samantha would listen to scratchy old records by the Beatles when they did their homework together. So Samantha *thought* they were going to do their homework!

'Why don't you sit down and we'll have some tea before we get our books. You were so late I made myself a pot.'

Sam didn't see anywhere he could sit. For that matter he didn't see tea cups or a teapot either.

He said, 'Well, I guess I'll just stand a while.'

Samantha smiled in that curious way, as if she was more confused than him. 'Green tea, Sammy?'

Sam said, 'Yeah, sure, why not?' and Samantha performed another mime: a teapot, a delicate cup on a plate, the pouring out.

She smiled and held out her empty hand.

'There you are,' she said, her slender hand stretched toward him. Sam didn't move a muscle. Samantha rolled her eyes. 'Please won't you take it, Sam? You know, I'm beginning to think you're afraid of me.'

Sam swallowed hard. He put out his shaking hand. He didn't let his fingers touch the ghostly Samantha's, but he did his best to mime. He took a tea cup on a tea plate right out of thin air. He wondered if there was an invisible biscuit too. He mimed a sip of green tea.

'It hasn't gone tepid?' Samantha asked.

'No,' Sam said. 'It's – delicious.'

'Oh. Good.'

No – bad! He was alive and Samantha was dead! Here she was talking to him as if nothing had ever happened, and she'd died one year ago to the day! Of course Sam had dreamed of Samantha and longed for Samantha, but he knew that she was dead. So why was all this happening now?

VENERO ARMANNO was born in Brisbane in 1959, and has studied at the University of Queensland, the Australian Film, Television and Radio School, Queensland University of Technology, and the Tisch School of the Arts, New York University. The son of Sicilian migrants, he has travelled and worked widely throughout the world. In 1995, 1997 and 1999 he lived and worked at the Cité Internationale des Arts, Paris, and he is frequently invited to speak about his work in Spain and Germany. He is the author of a book of adult short stories, *Jumping at the Moon*, and the adult novels *The Lonely Hunter*, *My Beautiful Friend* and *The Volcano*. His books for children include *The Ghost of Love Street* and *The Ghost of Deadman's Beach* for the Lothian *After Dark* series.

NET INSANITY

PAUL COLLINS

I'm a cyber junkie. So when I was invited to become a citizen of Cybercity, I jumped at the opportunity. The Artificial Intelligence that created Cybercity was a computer-generated program that could actually think for itself. I never could resist new technology.

I logged on as 'Rollerball' and joined the chat list. There were spaced-out names on that list: Snow_Ogre, Rogue-9 and Coolgirl3.

The chat was bizarre. Snow_Ogre posted a message to me straight away:

>Cybercity's got a virus, Rollerball. Get out now<

Rogue-9 added >Rollerball, don't answer. Just quit<

I grinned. What a pack of nerds. Trying to scare off the newbie in town. I typed my own message: >I'm here to stay, guys. I like your town<

I signed off and clicked on to the main menu. I figured the Artificial Intelligence would have the best-designed house in Cybercity, so clicked on 'visit AI plaza'.

This website was *weird*. The AI wanted me to sign away parts of my body! Talk about 'cutting edge' technology! My left arm was worth one hundred points, which gave me a password to enter the sprawling apartment building. My right arm was worth one hundred and fifty points, and those points combined with the points from my left arm gave me a master password for every apartment. For my head, the AI would let me meet anyone in Cybercity, including those dags Snow_Ogre and Rogue-9. My feet were worth two hundred points, and they, coupled with one hundred points, bought me an apartment.

I happily signed away. In real life I know body parts are worth a small fortune – in fact people even get kidnapped and have parts of their anatomy *stolen*. But this was virtual reality. It was only a game.

It cost me my right hand for an avatar, which is a virtual icon of myself. I strolled down the wind-swept streets of the virtual city. Laser signs stabbed into the darkness and reflected eerily off the rain-splattered streetscape.

I stumbled and noticed that my right foot had disappeared. There was no blood of course – avatars don't leak blood. I hobbled a few paces and fell. Hands outstretched, I landed on the stumps of my wrists. Gone! I was fading fast. What a dud game!

Back in real time I suddenly felt a massive headache coming on, and a stinging sensation in my hands.

'Spooky,' I said to myself and tried to quit. But my hands were lifeless. I thumped down on the quit icon anyway. That's when an electrical current zapped me.

'Yeow!' I screamed. Dazed, I watched my avatar walk straight into a brick wall. Things started getting blurry then, and I screamed for help.

A girl in a luminescent green jumpsuit and metallic headgear led a group of avatars into the plaza.

'It's okay, Rollerball,' a girl's voice said. 'Snow_Ogre to the rescue!' She was furiously typing into a miniature mobile phone. 'The anti virus program isn't working!' she screamed. 'I need backup.'

There was backup. Avatars quickly produced keyboards and began entering data.

Something large loomed from the darkness. It drank the light and swallowed entire buildings.

Its shadow fell on us. I was helpless now. Both my legs and one hand were missing. My face was blurring as the AI swept over me. I swirled around as though caught in a vortex.

In real time, my vision swam in and out of focus. The computer screen jumped away from me then slid sideways.

'It's working!' Snow_Ogre yelled. 'We're pushing it back!'

Lights from windows sprang on as the dark force of the AI swept back across the cityscape.

'Get the newbie out of here!' Snow_Ogre ordered. 'He's almost gone. Quick about it!'

Suddenly I felt hands lift me into the air. In real time my body jerked about as though it were being carried across rough country. I was fading fast as the virtual people carried me to safety.

I woke in real time. It was late. Even the screen-saver had cut out. I touched the mouse and Cybercity came back on line. My hands felt numb, as though they'd been in casts for years. I tried to stretch but my limbs ached. I ran my fingers through my hair. Everything seemed so *unfamiliar*.

That's when my thoughts were shunted aside by some force far stronger than me. I watched helplessly as my fingers started tapping.

>Snow_Ogre? You online? Coolgirl3? Rogue-9?<

The chat list scrolled down. Snow_Ogre answered.

>Hey, Rollerball. You gotta watch that AI. It's . . . we dunno. We think it's out to do something bad. We've alerted Net Security but got no answer. Be careful<

Frozen with fear, I realised I was no longer in control. The AI had somehow taken over my mind in real time.

>Thanks for the warning, Snow_Ogre< my fingers typed. >Please meet me in the plaza. I have a plan. Rollerball<

Numbly, I watched the Cybercity people crowd into the plaza. The AI was after parts, human parts. Where better to buy what you need than on the Net . . .

PAUL COLLINS' books for younger readers include *Swords of Quentaris, Slaves of Quentaris*, and the best-selling fantasy novel, *Dragonlinks*. He has been short-listed for many Australian literary awards, and has won the Aurealis for speculative fiction, the inaugural Peter McNamara, and the William Atheling Awards. Paul has a black belt in both taekwondo and jujitsu and, many of Paul's martial arts experiences can be found in books such as *Sneila*, a recent title from Penguin Australia.

FLESH AND BLOOD

Excerpt from *Rowan of Rin*
EMILY RODDA

To the sturdy villagers of Rin the boy Rowan is a timid weakling. The most disappointing child ever. Yet, incredibly, it is his help they need when the stream that flows from the top of the Mountain dries up. Without its water their precious bukshah herds will die, and Rin will be doomed. The six strongest villagers must brave the unknown terrors of the Mountain to discover the answer to the riddle. And Rowan, the unwanted seventh member of the group, must go with them.

Marlie and Rowan ran towards the sound of Val's voice. John followed, dragging Allun, who was still struggling but starting to look confused instead of angry.

They found Val lying face down in a clump of reeds, her feet on solid ground but her body in the mud, her arms around Bronden's waist. And Bronden was fighting her. Silently and determinedly fighting to be free – stretching her fingers out to something only she could see, while the swamp pulled her down.

'She suddenly called out, and plunged away into the mud,' gasped Val. 'I cannot pull her back. She will not listen to me. Oh, if Ellis were here. I – I cannot think without him.'

Marlie pulled a coil of rope from her pack. 'Hold me, Rowan,' she called, and flung herself down to lie beside Val.

Rowan held Marlie's ankles and watched her stretch across the reeds, reaching for Bronden. Marlie was tall, but not as tall as Val. As she crawled further out into the mud, Rowan was pulled forward, until he too was lying on his belly across the pathway. His muscles strained as Marlie pushed her hands under Val's and looped the rope around Bronden's belt. Val, too, groaned. She had been bearing Bronden's weight for so long. She would not be able to hold on much longer.

'Back! Rowan – try to pull me back, now,' shouted Marlie. 'Can you do it?'

Rowan heaved with all his might, but Marlie was heavy, and her ankles were slippery with mud. To his horror he felt his hands beginning to lose their grip. 'John,' he shrieked in desperation. 'Help Marlie! I can't . . .'

'Marlie!' There was a scuffle behind him. Then two slim, strong hands had come down on top of his own, and Allun's voice was calling, 'I have you, Marlie,' as he heaved her to safety, with the rope that was Bronden's lifeline clutched in her hand.

It took all three of them to haul Bronden back, while Val lay exhausted on the ground and Rowan stood helplessly by. The mud was holding fast to its victim, and Bronden herself was fighting them. Even when they had her safe at their feet she was moaning and crying, trying to crawl back into the ooze that had nearly swallowed her for ever.

'Minna,' she was weeping. 'Minna, Minna, Minna!'

'Who is Minna?' Rowan whispered to Strong John. He had heard the name before, but he could not think where. 'Who did Bronden see?'

John was shaking his head sadly, looking down at the crying woman. 'I had forgotten little Minna,' he said. 'I had forgotten all about her, until Bronden became so angry with you for thinking of the bukshah. And I think, except in a secret part of her mind, Bronden had almost forgotten her too. But this place . . .'

'When we were all children, Rowan,' said Allun, 'and I still new to Rin, Bronden had a friend. One friend. Minna, the keeper of bukshah in those days. A little girl as quiet and gentle and fearful as Bronden was loud and bullying and fearless. They were never apart. For Minna, there was only Bronden and the bukshah. For Bronden, there was only Minna.'

'I remember Minna,' said Marlie softly. 'And so would your mother, Rowan. We all went out looking for her – even the children – the night she disappeared.'

Bronden groaned, and looked up at Val, who was bending over her anxiously. 'Minna is here, Val,' she croaked. 'I saw her. I heard her voice. I felt her hand on my face. But Val –' her strong face crumpled, and tears fell from her eyes, 'Val, she is still a little girl. She has never grown up. She has been wandering here all these years, all alone. Why did you not let me go to her?'

Strong John knelt down beside her. 'Minna died, Bronden,' he said gently. 'They found her bones, at last, and the bones of the calf she was trying to save, in the old mineshaft. You remember.'

Rowan stared. Minna had been quiet and shy, like him. Minna had died, seeking a lost bukshah. Was that why . . .

'We do not know that that was Minna, with the calf,' Bronden moaned. 'We do not know for sure. I have always wondered . . .'

John stroked her forehead. His face was full of pity. 'Minna is dead, Bronden. Minna is safe, and resting in the graveyard. The spirits of the swamp played a terrible trick on you, to make you leave the firm ground. As they did with Rowan and his bukshah. And tried to do with Allun and his mother.'

'I do not believe in such things,' Bronden looked around her with terrified eyes. 'And yet you must speak truly, for Minna cannot be ten years old still. But I saw her. I felt her. I heard her.' She gripped Strong John's hands. 'John! Do not let them touch me again! Do not let me hear them! I could not bear it.' She struggled to her feet. The mist billowed around her, and she started like a frightened animal.

'Come along, Bronden,' said Strong John, still in that gentle voice. 'Come along.' He began to lead her on.

'No!' Bronden dug in her toes, her eyes black with fear. 'No! I cannot!'

'Bronden, you must come!'

'No!' She tore away from him, panting, then turned and began to run back the way they had come, her thumbs over her ears, her hands blinkering her eyes.

'Bronden,' shrieked Val. 'Come back!'

But Bronden did not turn or hesitate. Soon she was out of sight.

Now we are five, thought Rowan.

EMILY RODDA, one of Australia's most successful, popular and versatile writers, has won the Children's Book Council of Australia Book of the Year Award five times. A former editor of *The Women's Weekly,* Emily is also the best-selling author of adult mysteries under her own name of Jennifer Rowe. Her children's books, for a range of ages and genres, exhibit a mastery of plot and character. Her many books include *Finders Keepers* and *The Timekeeper* (both serialised for television); *Crumbs!*; *Rowan of Rin*; *Rowan and the Travellers*; *Rowan and the Keeper of the Crystal*; *Rowan and the Zebak*; and *Rowan of the Bukshah*, all published by Omnibus Books. *Teen Power Inc*, a mystery adventure series Emily wrote for young readers, attracts an enthusiastic and devoted following. Emily's *Deltora Quest* series has as its storyline a perilous quest involving three heroes who have to find all the gems that make up a magic belt and has touched the imaginations of children everywhere. *The Rowan of Rin* series, first launched in 1993 and now re-released, is loved by children and adults alike. Each book is a complete story and centres on the series' unlikely hero, Rowan of Rin.

DOUBLE SORROW

Excerpt from *Ghostop Book One*
LIBBY HATHORN

Juliet was filled with pity for this poor, tortured girl. It was terrible, surely the most terrible death she could have imagined. She knew now why the ghost of Rose Cottage could not find peace.

'I'll try to set it right for you,' she whispered, 'dear Rosette, who died in such a vile way under the swamp. There's no shame at all in what you did. Only tell me how I can help you. And whoever Flo is, I'll help you both.' And there were more tears at the thought of this grisly death and the realisation she was the privileged one who'd at last been contacted from the spirit world.

As she dried her tears she knew she had to tell someone to dampen the rush of feelings that assailed her. Georgia! She turned to her computer. At last there was a message from her sister. Reading Georgia's words served to slow her racing heartbeat.

To: julietsunday@infinet.net.au
From: georgsunday@delaferriere.com

> Dear Juliet
> I'm online, my dear, at last and I've just caught up with all your frantic messages—ta!
> The chateau is fab, though Dad doesn't think so. It's broken down and beguilingly beautiful. Will send photos. Dad's out and about doing business and quiet as ever at home.
> It sounds amazing, Juliet, what's happening with you at Nan's place. Look, it's crazy but, to tell the truth, I have some problems of my own in that department (the ghostly one). A few weird happenings of our own in the cellar that's underneath us. Not to mention the gigantic attic rooms up top and the place they call the Widow's Walk. The past hangs on here too in ghostly associations, though Dad denies it (being Dad).
> Miss you and wish you were here, but as twins, we're still mirroring each other . . . It seems we've both alighted at Ghost Stops, wouldn't you say?
> I'm glad Mario's on the scene. No talent to speak of here yet! But I'm hoping. We've been invited to a neighbour's who has three sons . . . hmm. I'll ask them about our ghosts.
> Don't fret, pet! Remember ghosts can always be sent back! Just tell 'em loud and clear. I've found this invaluable advice myself.
> Keep me informed and I'll write at length later.
> Georgia.

Juliet pressed the return mail key but the computer buzzed with an unusual sound and she remembered the storm warning. Should turn it off or there'd be another technical hitch. She was bursting with this story, simply had to talk with someone close. Oh why not Mario? Why not? She'd break the rule and phone him, though. She simply had to . . . She was poised to hang up but mercifully it was his voice.

'I know how she died! I know!' Juliet told him, almost in tears again.

'Who?' he sounded annoyed with her but she had to speak to him. Just had to. It seemed unutterably important.

'Rosette. It's a long story –'

'Listen, Juliet, I don't want to know any stories at ten

o'clock at night. I've told you not to phone here. Not ever.'

'But, Mario, I had to speak to you tonight. I had to! It's important –' her voice broke. 'I'm so excited about her story – but all of this frightens me!'

'Jules, I'm sorry to sound so angry –' his tone softened, 'and I do want to hear your ghost story. But not now. If anyone in this house overhears this conversation, it's fatal! We're done, you know that!'

They both heard the click of a receiver, as if on cue.

'God almighty, that'll be Sergio! You've done it now. I'd better go!' His voice was dark with anger.

What had she done? And why was he such a captive in his own house? Now she felt furious. She was filled to the brim with thoughts of Rosette and he'd refused to hear or to help. To even ask if she needed help!

It was some hours before Juliet could sleep. And when she did, thoughts of crossed and dripping limestone caves, of manacles and tombstones, plagued her dreams. She woke up to the sound of wind whipping up outside. She was sure she'd heard something – maybe that wretched moaning again, the double sorrow chant. Sitting upright she strained to hear, and there was the distant echo of laughter. Laughter? A cascade of it followed and it was coming from the attic, she was sure. Cruel and mocking laughter. She found she couldn't move and she couldn't speak. 'Mario!' she wanted to scream out as if she was aware of the imminent loss of him once more. 'Oh, Mario!'

The laughter gradually died away, but as it did, Juliet felt really afraid of what she was undertaking in this house. It seemed as if all the tantalising clues, the cemetery, the heartrending story she'd just read, all of it had entangled her in some hideously clever way with that inexplicable evil!

Suddenly, there was an indrawn breath in the room, and not her own! She wanted to put her hands over her ears so she would not, could not hear the voice she dreaded would speak out any moment. Say something so bad it would change her life forever. Her limbs remained motionless but as a tear trickled down her cheek she realised she could speak.

'Nan!' she croaked. But she knew she'd have to stem the evil in some way herself. And then Georgia's advice sprang to mind. 'Just tell 'em loud and clear.' Well, she would. But what to say? A chant? Love poems were of no use, but that's all that sprang to mind. Then it came to her.

'Speak no evil!' she warned, her voice strong with anger. 'You monstrous darkling things. Speak no evil! Hear me! And you be gone from here. I don't want you hanging around me any more!'

The silence deepened for long, dreadful moments. There seemed to be a rush of wings outside, like birds leaving shelter. And then there was the sound of a sudden downpour, a thrumming on the tin roof of the verandah outside. And with it a sweet relief.

Juliet jumped from her bed and drew her dressing-gown around her. No crash of thunder, no streaks of lightning out there – just good, old-fashioned, healthy-sounding rain. The terrible feeling had lifted miraculously but was immediately replaced with anxiety. What in the hell was really going on here? Should she be digging and delving where everybody was telling her not to go? And who could she turn to now?

'Georgia,' she whispered and in moments, despite the storm, the computer was humming.

To: georgsunday@delaferriere.com
From: julietsunday@infinet.net.au
I'm okay now but I've had a terrible fright, Georgia dear. Rose Cottage, as you so rightly said, is surely a ghostop! My hands are still a bit shakey as I type. But I must tell someone and you're it!

Please give me some instant feedback. I need it right now, I really do. You see I think I've messed up well and good with Mario this time. Not me, exactly. It may be that a ghost has come between us. I'm really freaked by what's going on as I'm not quite sure myself. But tonight I felt its evil intent in this room, and it was horrible.

I'm going to do my best to try and explain everything to you . . . someone's got to help me out of this mess!

Something made Juliet gaze up a moment at the rain-wet window. She started. Eyes. Lurid-green changing to mustard-yellow eyes stared in at her – ambient, horrifying! Eyes that did not for one second break their searching gaze. They seemed to bore into her very soul. She tried to look away but somehow could not. They were hypnotic pools of liquid evil! Who – what was it?

She drew in her breath to scream but for the second time that night, Juliet Sunday found she could make no sound.

LIBBY HATHORN was born in Newcastle and brought up in the Sydney suburbs of Maroubra and Tamarama Beach. The beach and the bush had a great influence on her childhood, also helped shape much of her adult writing. *Looking out for Sampson*, a short novel for young readers, is set on Bondi Beach; as is one of her earliest picture storybooks, *The Tram to Bondi Beach*. Another Sydney beach, Coogee, features in her novel *Love Me Tender*. And *Thunderwith* – her first young adult novel – is set in the heart of a New South Wales semi-tropical forest, the Wallingat. Nowadays, Libby has a grown-up family but her children, Lisa and Keiran, featured in some of her books when they were little kids.

LIST OF AUTHORS

Alexander, Goldie · 36
Armanno, Venero · 138
Ball, Duncan · 18
Bell, Anita · 73, 77
Blackford, Jenny · 41
Brian, Janeen · 106
Clark, Margaret · 31
Collins, Paul · 143
Farrer, Vashti · 68
Fienberg, Anna and Barbara · 24
Griffiths, Andy · 1
Jennings, Paul · 82
Jinks, Catherine · 112
Harris, Christine · 91

Hathorn, Libby · 152
Hilton, Nette · 50
Hutchins, Elizabeth · 95
Ingram, Anne · 126, 129
Kelleher, Victor · 59
Killeen, Gretel · 9
Marsden, John · 13
Masson, Sophie · 55
McDonald, Meme · 117
Park, Ruth · 132
Pryor, Boori Monty · 117
Pulman, Felicity · 46
Rodda, Emily · 147
Wignell, Edel · 101
Wrightson, Patricia · 121

ACKNOWLEDGEMENTS

1. Extract from *Just Tricking* by Andy Griffiths reprinted by permission of Pan Macmillan Australia Pty Ltd. Text Copyright © Andy Griffiths 1997.

2. Extract from *My Sister's a Nightmare* by Gretel Killeen reprinted by permission of Random House Australia Pty Ltd. Text and Illustrations Copyright © Gretel Killeen 2000.

3. Extract from *Cool School* by John Marsden reprinted by permission of Pan Macmillan Australia Pty Ltd. Copyright © John Mardsen 1995.

4. Extract from *Emily Eyefinger and the Ghost Ship* by Duncan Ball reprinted by permission of Harper Collins Publishers. Text Copyright © Duncan Ball 2004.

5. Extract from *The Big, Big, Big Book of Tashi* by Anna and Barbara Fienberg reprinted by permission of Allen & Unwin. Text Copyright © Anna and Barbara Fienberg 1996.

6. Extract from *Murder on the Ghoul Bus* by Margaret Clark reprinted by permission of Random House Australia Pty Ltd. Copyright © Margaret Clark/Lee Striker 1997.

7. *Liar Ghost* by Goldie Alexander reproduced by permission of Goldie Alexander. Copyright © Goldie Alexander 2004.

8. *Alistair* by Jenny Blackford reproduced by permission of Jenny Blackford. Copyright © Jenny Blackford 2004.

9. Extract from *Ghost Boy* by Felicity Pulman reprinted by permission of Random House Australia Pty Ltd. Copyright © Felicity Pulman 2004.

10. Extract from *A Ghost of a Chance* by Nette Hilton reprinted by permission of Penguin Australia. Text Copyright © Nette Hilton 1998.

11. *She Just Wants to Play* by Sophie Masson reproduced by permission of Sophie Masson, care of Margaret Connolly & Associates Pty Ltd. Copyright © Sophie Masson 2004.

12. *Dragon's Tooth* by Victor Kelleher reproduced by permission of Victor Kelleher, care of Margaret Connolly & Associates Pty Ltd. Copyright © Victor Kelleher 2004.

13. *Past Lives* by Vashti Farrer first published in NSW School Magazine, *Orbit*, February 2002, reproduced by permission of Vashti Farrer. Copyright © Vashti Farrer 2002.

14. *Fluff on the Brain* by Anita Bell reproduced by permission of Anita Bell, author *Crystal Coffin* and the *Kirby's Crusaders* series. Copyright © Anita Bell 2004.

15. *Voices from Beyond* by Anita Bell reproduced by permission of Anita Bell, author *Crystal Coffin* and the *Kirby's Crusaders* series. Copyright © Anita Bell 2004.

ACKNOWLEDGEMENTS

16. Extract from *Unbelievable!* by Paul Jennings reprinted by permission of Penguin Australia. Text Copyright © Lockley Lodge Pty Ltd 1986.
17. 'The Haunting of Clayton Quinn' from *Party Animals* by Christine Harris reprinted by permission of Random House Australia Pty Ltd. Copyright © Christine Harris 1996.
18. *The Scent of Violets* by Elizabeth Hutchins first published in *Spinouts Sapphire: Shadowlands*, Pearson Education Australia, reproduced by permission of Elizabeth Hutchins. Copyright © Elizabeth Hutchins 2002.
19. *Federici is Not a Cat* by Edel Wignell adapted from a story first published in NSW School Magazine, *Orbit*, 2002, reproduced by permission of Edel Wignell. Copyright © Edel Wignell 2002.
20. *Dead or Alive* by Janeen Brian first published in NSW School Magazine, *Orbit*, August 2002, reproduced by permission of Janeen Brian. Copyright © Janeen Brian 2002.
21. Extract from *Eloise* by Catherine Jinks reprinted by permission of Allen & Unwin. Copyright © Catherine Jinks 2003.
22. Extract from *The Binna Binna Man* by Meme McDonald and Boori Monty Pryor reprinted by permission of Allen & Unwin. First published by Allen & Unwin Australia 1999. Copyright © Meme McDonald and Boori Monty Pryor 1999.
23. Extract from *The Nargun and the Stars* by Patricia Wrightson reprinted by permission of Penguin Australia. Copyright © Patricia Wrightson 1973.
24. 'The White Bull' from *Shudders and Shakes* retold from various sources by Anne Ingram, reproduced by permission of Anne Ingram. Copyright © William Collins 1972.
25. 'The Black Horse of Sutton' from *Shudders and Shakes* retold from various sources by Anne Ingram, reproduced by permission of Anne Ingram. Copyright © William Collins 1972.
26. Extract from *Playing Beatie Bow* by Ruth Park reprinted by permission of Penguin Australia. Copyright © Ruth Park 1980.
27. Extract from *The Ghost of Love Street* by Venero Armanno reprinted by permission of Lothian Books. Copyright © Venero Armanno 1997.
28. *Net Insanity* by Paul Collins first published in *Challenge* magazine, Issue 4, 2000, reproduced by permission of Paul Collins. Copyright © Paul Collins 2000.
29. Extract from *Rowan of Rin* by Emily Rodda. First published by Omnibus Books, a division of Scholastic Australia Pty Ltd, 1993. Reproduced by permission of Scholastic Australia Pty Ltd. Text Copyright © Emily Rodda 1993.
30. Extract from *Ghostop Book One: Double Sorrow* by Libby Hathorn reprinted by permission of Hodder Headline Australia. Copyright © Hathorn Enterprises Ltd 1999.

LINSAY KNIGHT

Linsay Knight is widely respected as a leading expert in, and contributor to, Australian children's literature. As the Managing Editor and Children's Book Publisher at Random House Australia for ten years, Linsay nurtured the talent of numerous authors and illustrators to create some of Australia's most successful children's books.

Linsay is also the author of several successful children's books in *The Macquarie Beginner Book* series and is the co-author of titles such as *The Macquarie Young Kids' Dictionary* and *The Dictionary of Performing Arts in Australia* Volumes 1 and 2. She edited *30 Australian Stories for Children* in 2003.

GREGORY ROGERS

Gregory Rogers studied fine art at the Queensland College of Art and has illustrated a large number of educational and trade children's picture books.

In 1995, Gregory won the Kate Greenaway Medal for his illustrations in *Way Home*. *Way Home* also won a parents' Choice Award in the US and was shortlisted for the ABPA book design awards.

Gregory's most recent picture books include *Beyond the Dusk* by Victor Kelleher, *The Gift* by Libby Hathorn and *Princess Max* by Laurie Stiller for Random House Australia. He illustrated *30 Australian Stories for Children* in 2003.